Get Set for The Code 2nd Edition B

A primer for the **Explode The Code**® *series*

EDUCATORS PUBLISHING SERVICE
Cambridge and Toronto

Cover art: Hugh Price

Mayfield, PA, in May 2017
ISBN 978-0-8388-7820-0

3 4 5 PAH 19 18 17

Color or mark the one that is different.

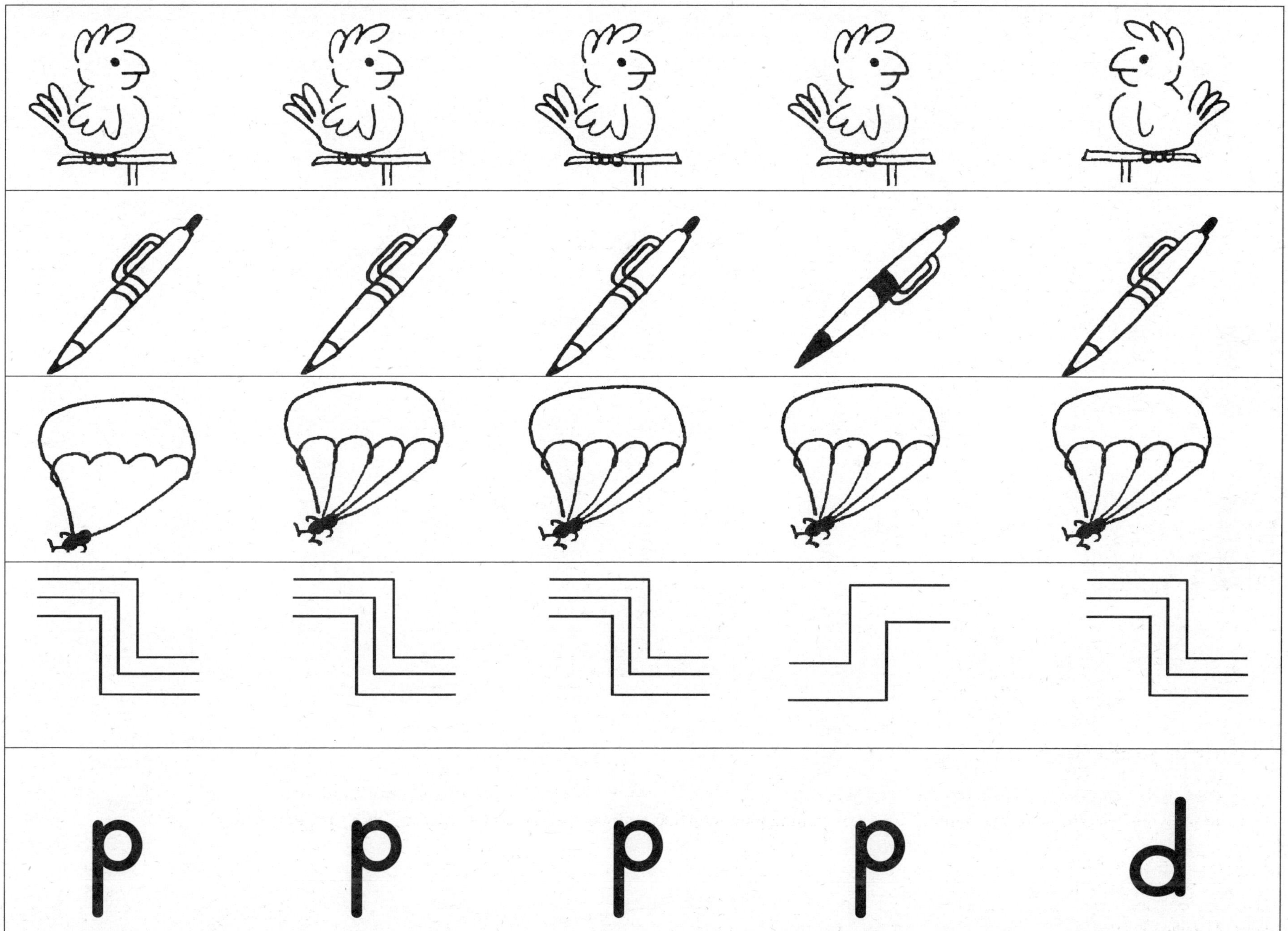

Trace the letter **p** with your finger. This letter has the sound you hear at the beginning of 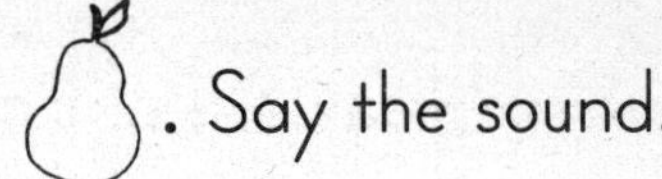. Say the sound.

1

p

2

Capital letters are used
to begin sentences and names.
A capital **p** looks like this: P.
Capital letters are two spaces tall.

Pp

Put your pencil on **p.** Follow the path to the picture. Say the sound. Try not to cross any lines.

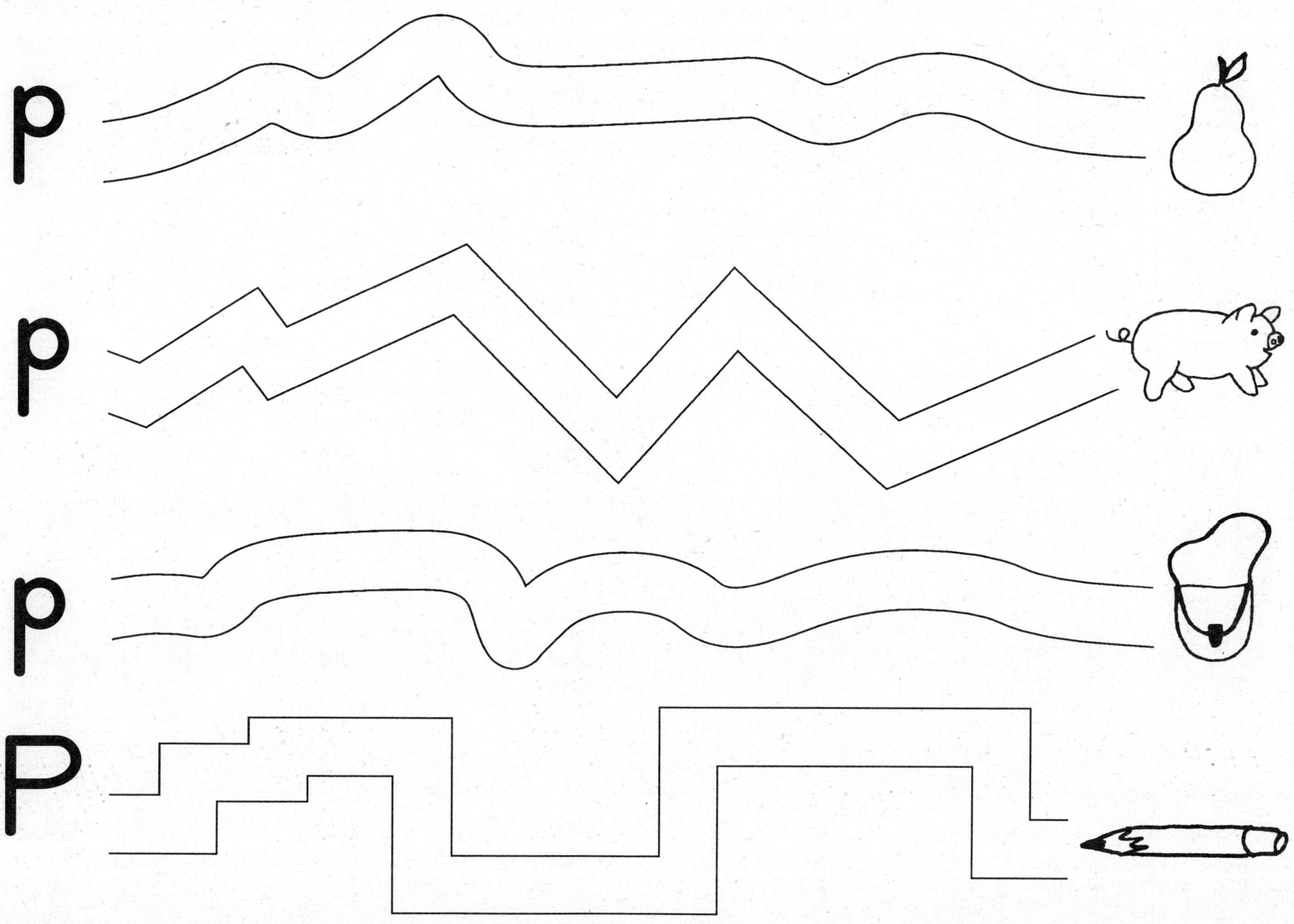

Look carefully at the letter in the box. Circle the letters that match it.

p	m	p	k	b	p
k	k	b	k	r	k
p	p	r	m	p	p
r	p	r	k	r	m
P	B	P	P	F	P

Say the name of the picture. Now say the sound that comes at the beginning of 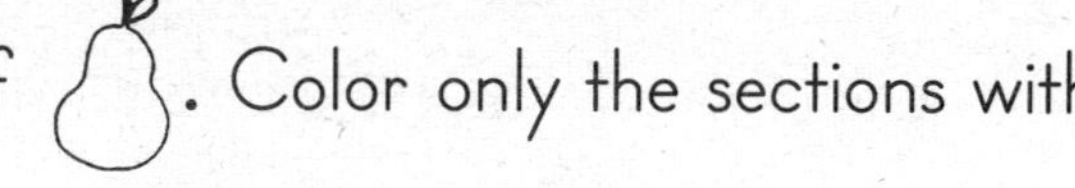. Color only the sections with the letter **p** or P in them.

p t f m p

k r P k T

p

F r

m

P m

Pp

Teacher: Read the directions aloud while the students listen and work on page 7.

1. I am thinking of something that tastes delicious. It has a crust and is baked in the oven. When you cut it into slices everyone in the family can have a piece. I am thinking of a _____ [pie]. Put your finger on the **pie.** What sound do you hear at the beginning of **pie?** Color the **pie** red.

2. I am thinking of something you use to write your name. It sometimes has an eraser on the end. What is it? [pencil] Put your finger on the **pencil.** What sound does **pencil** begin with? Color the **pencil** blue.

3. Now I am thinking of an animal. It is sometimes pink, and loves to lie in the mud. What is it? [pig] Put your finger on the **pig.** What sound does **pig** begin with? Draw mud around the **pig's** feet.

4. This juicy and delicious fruit grows on a tree. It is either brown or greenish yellow when it is ripe. This fruit is rounded at one end and smaller at the other end. What is this fruit called? [pear] Put your finger on the **pear.** What sound does **pear** begin with? Put a big X on the **pear.**

5. Find something on this page that you wear to cover your legs. Sometimes we call them trousers, but usually we call them ____ [pants]. Put your finger on the **pants.** What sound does **pants** begin with? Color the pockets on the **pants.**

6. When you want to create a beautiful, colorful picture, you might use these. You use a brush and water with them. What are they called? [paints] Put your finger on the **paints.** What sound do you hear at the beginning of **paints?** Draw two circles around the **paints.**

7. There is one picture left. Look at it. This is something people can keep their money in. What is it? [purse] Put your finger on the **purse.** Draw a wider strap on the **purse** so it won't fall off your shoulder.

Listen; then follow the directions.

Draw a line from the letter **p** to each picture whose name begins with /**p**/ as in .

Follow the arrows to write the letter **p**, which says /**p**/as in pear. Say the sound aloud.

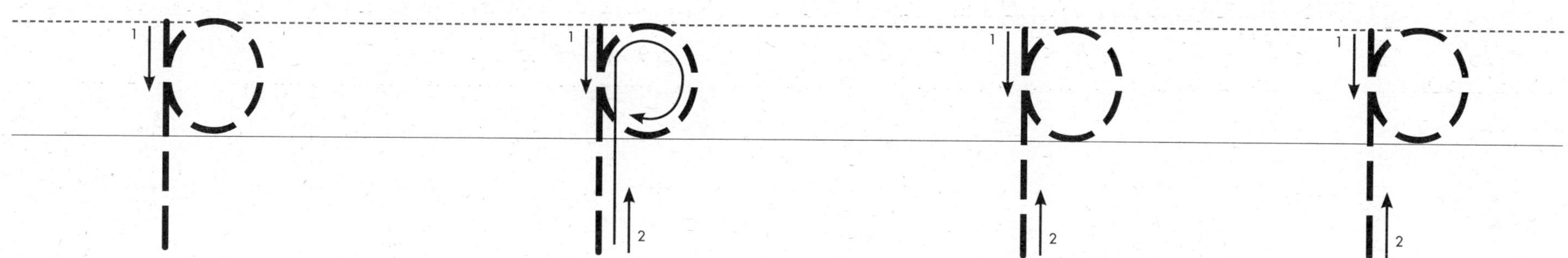

Notice that **p** hangs below the line. Trace the letters.

Color each picture whose name begins with **p** as in .

p		
p		
p		

Trace the letters.

p p p p p

Copy the letter.

p

(oval) each picture whose name begins with **p.** Write **p** below those pictures.

Draw a line from the picture to the letter that begins its name.

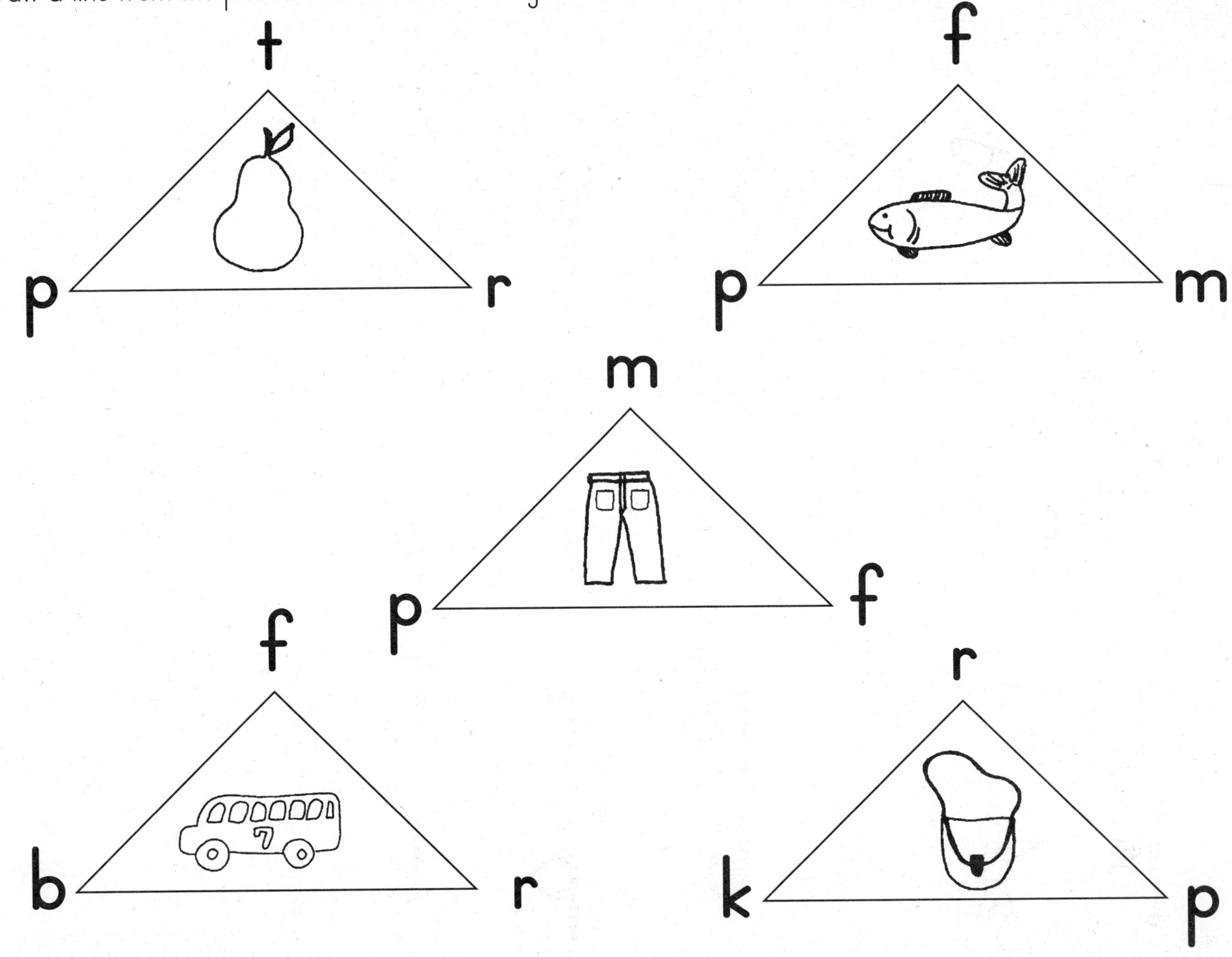

Say the name of the picture and the sound of its first letter.	Find the letter. Circle it.			Write the letter.
	f	p	b	
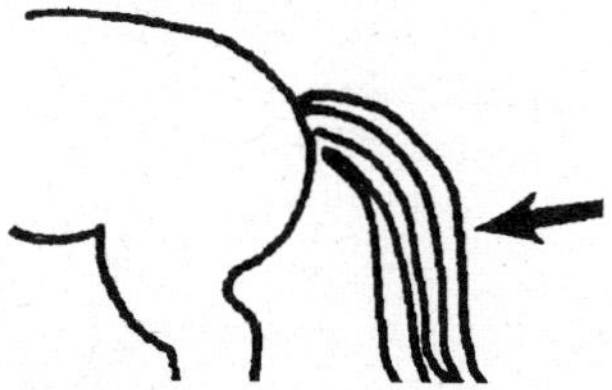	k	m	t	
	r	t	p	
	p	r	f	
	b	p	k	

Which sound does the word begin with? Write the letter that stands for the sound.

Color or mark the one that is different.

Trace the letter **s** with your finger. This letter has the sound you hear at the beginning of [sock]. Say the sound.

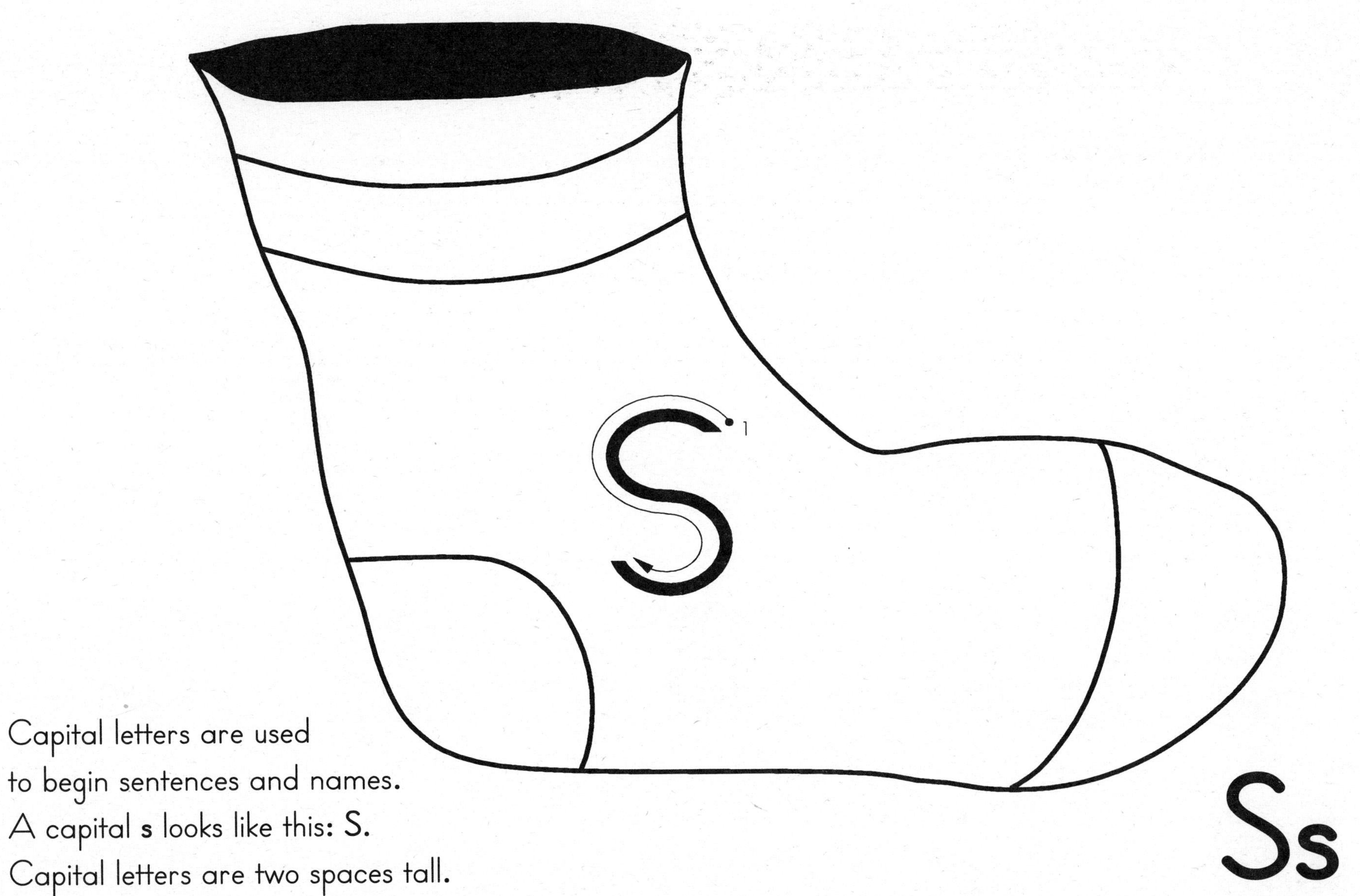

Capital letters are used
to begin sentences and names.
A capital **s** looks like this: S.
Capital letters are two spaces tall.

Ss

Put your pencil on **s.** Follow the path to the picture. Say the sound. Try not to cross any lines.

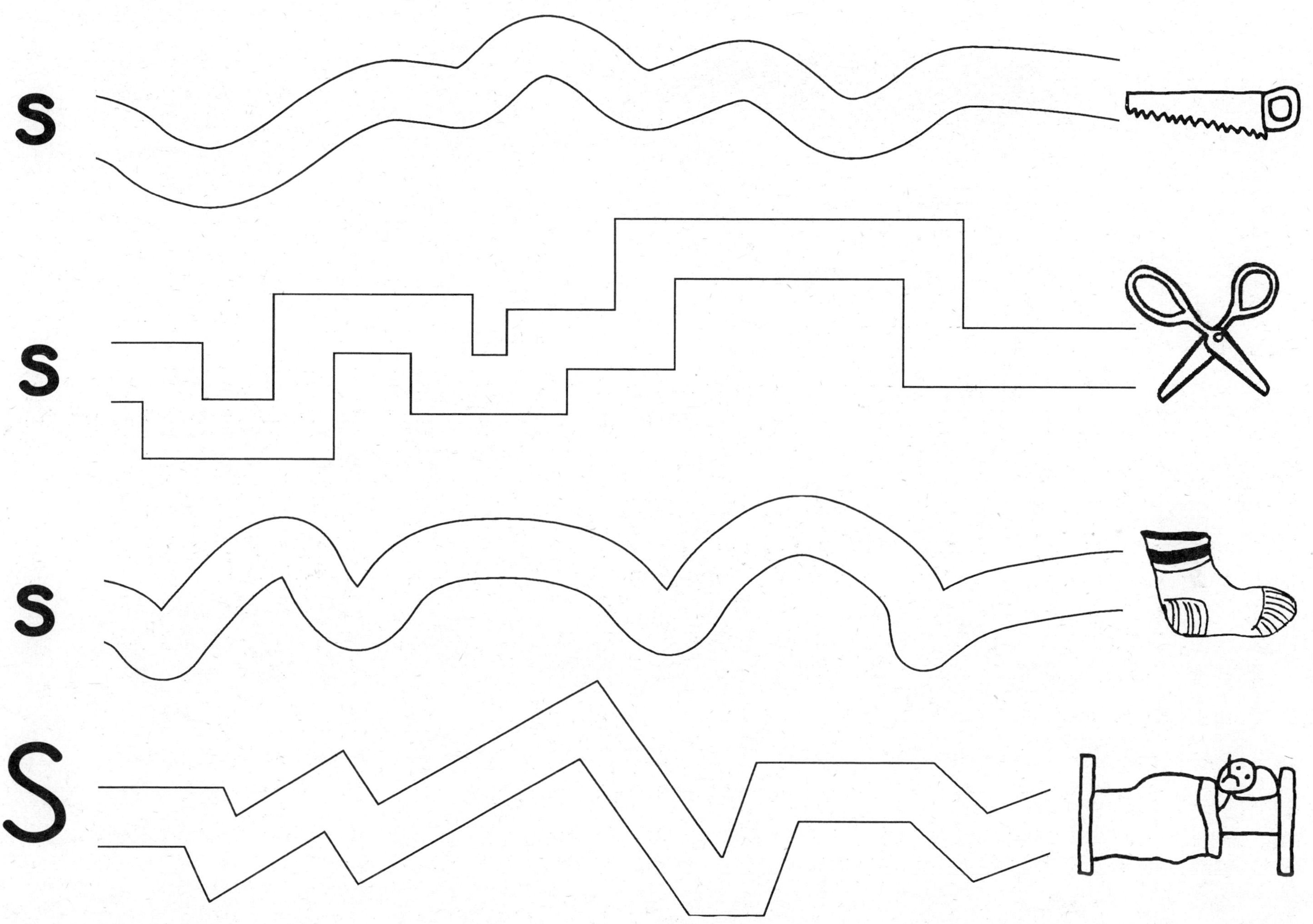

Look carefully at the letter in the box. Circle the letters that match it.

s	z	s	s	r	s
s	s	m	f	t	s
p	o	p	p	b	p
m	n	m	r	s	m
S	S	F	S	R	S

Say the name of the picture. Now say the sound that comes at the beginning of [sock]. Color only the sections with the letter **s** or S in them.

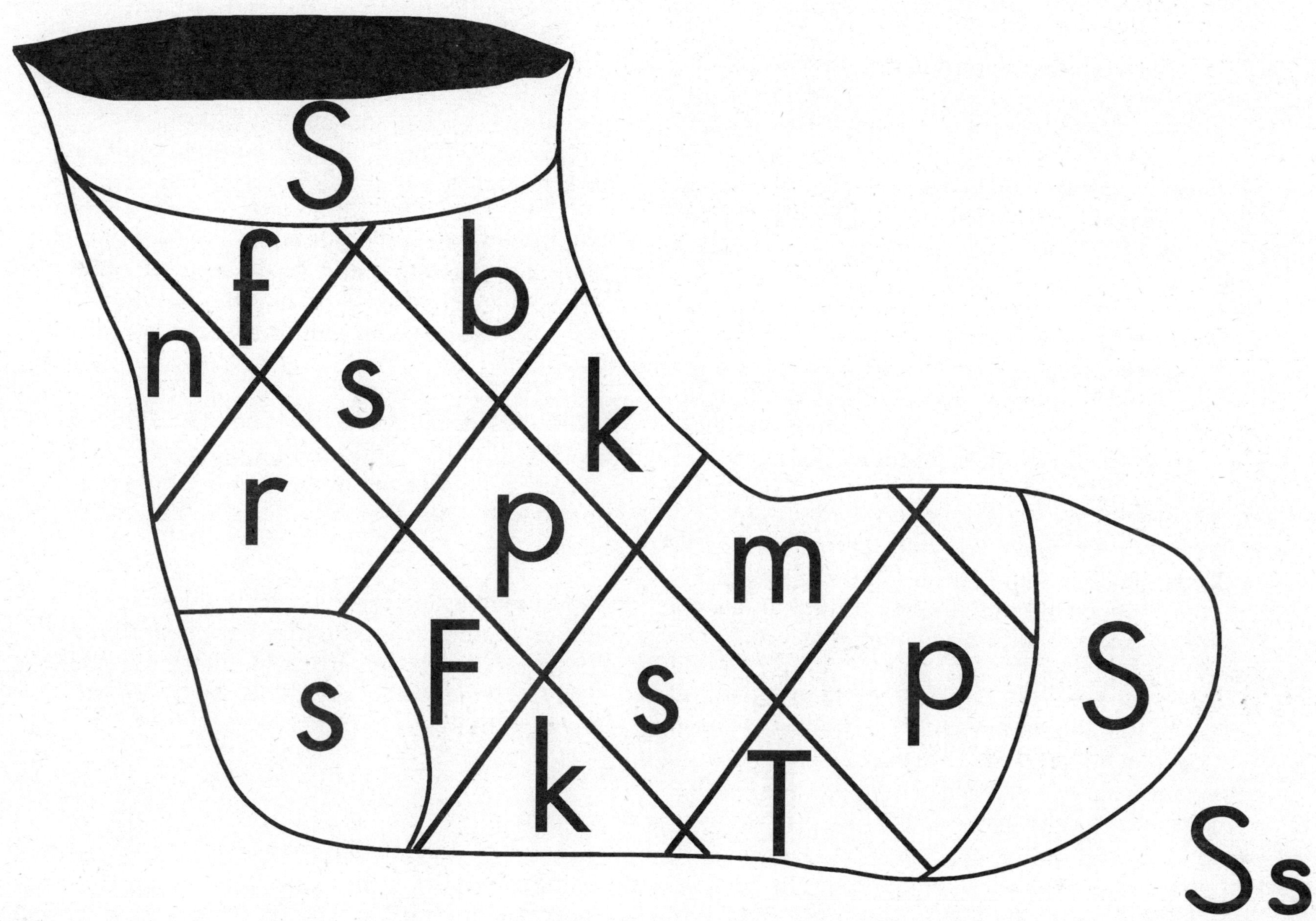

Teacher: Read the directions aloud while the students listen and work on page 21.

1. I am thinking of something that is good to eat, especially for lunch. It is easy to take on a picnic. It is made of two pieces of bread with filling between them. What am I thinking of? [sandwich] Put your finger on the **sandwich.** What sound do you hear at the beginning of **sandwich?** Color the filling in the **sandwich.**

2. I am thinking of something soft that you put on your foot before you put your shoe on. A pair of them helps keep your feet warm. Can you find what I am thinking of? [sock] Put your finger on the **sock.** What sound do you hear at the beginning of **sock?** Color the heel and toe of the **sock.**

3. When a day is not cloudy or rainy, you can see this in the sky. It is bright, and its light helps plants grow. What shines brightly in the daytime sky? [sun] Put your finger on the **sun.** What sound does **sun** begin with? Color the **sun** and add more sunbeams.

4. When you get in the car, you must buckle up so you will be safe. What do you buckle? [seat belt] Put your finger on the **seat belt.** Say **seat belt** and the sound you hear at the beginning of it. Draw a head on the person with a **seat belt.**

5. Find something on this page that you can use to cut paper. Be careful with them! What are they called? [scissors] Put your finger on the picture of the **scissors.** What sound do you hear at the beginning of **scissors?** Draw a circle around the **scissors.**

6. You can use this tool to cut wood. It is made of steel and has a wooden handle. What is it called? [saw] Put your finger on the picture of the **saw.** What sound does **saw** begin with? Draw a box around the **saw.**

7. When you are not feeling well and must go to bed, we say you are ____ [sick]. Put your finger on the picture of the **sick** person. What sound does **sick** begin with? Color the blanket on the **sick** person's bed.

8. Now I am thinking of something you wash your hands and face in. You also brush your teeth here because it has water and a drain. What is it? [sink] Put your finger on the **sink.** What sound does **sink** begin with? Draw lots of suds in the **sink.**

Listen; then follow the directions.

Draw a line from each picture to the letter that begins its name.

Follow the arrows to write the letter **s**, which says /**s**/as in [sock]. Say the sound aloud.

s s s s

Notice that **s** is only one space tall. Trace the letters.

s s s s

Which letter does the picture's name begin with? Circle it.

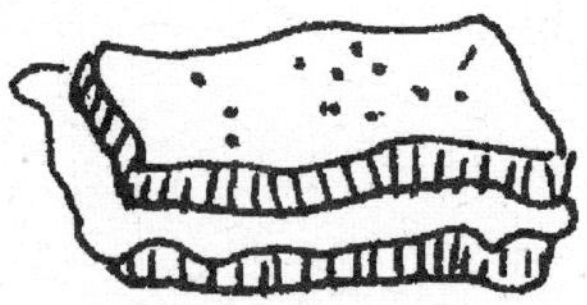 s r	 k f	 s p	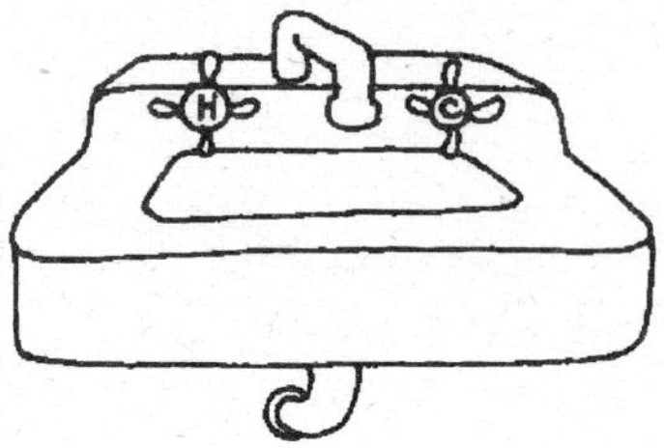 r s
 s f	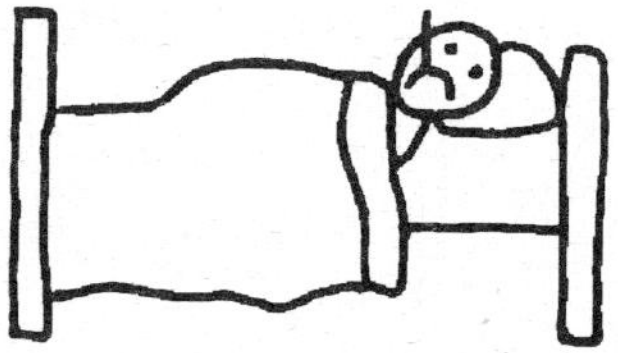 r s	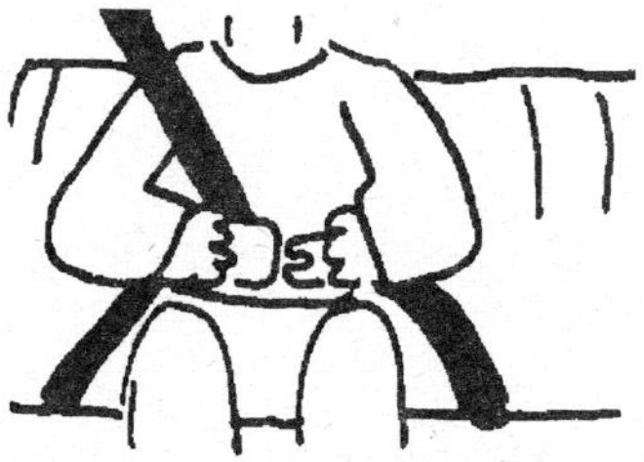 s k	 d t

Say the sound at the beginning of each pictured word.
Trace the letter that it begins with and write 2 more on the lines.

	t b	
	m r	
	s k	
	r p	

Say the sound of each letter. Then color the picture whose name begins with that sound.

s	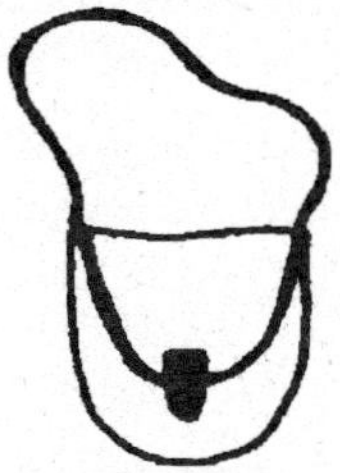		
s		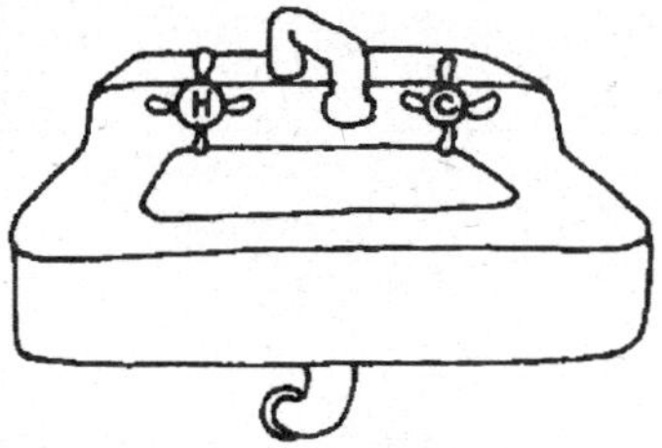	
b	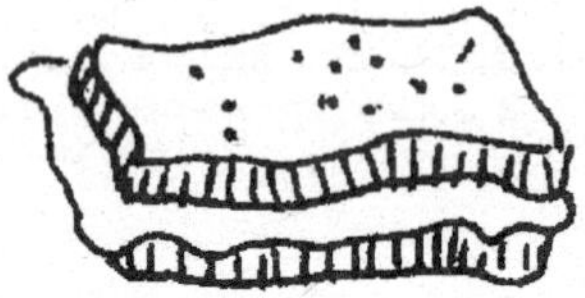		
s			
t		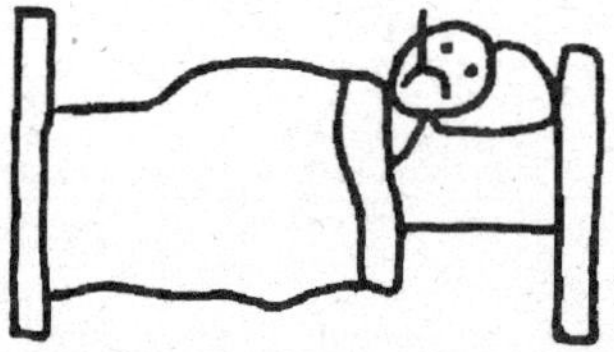	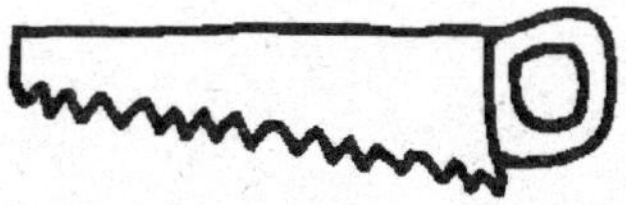

Say the name of the picture and the sound of its first letter.	Find the letter. Circle it.	Write the letter.
	k p s	
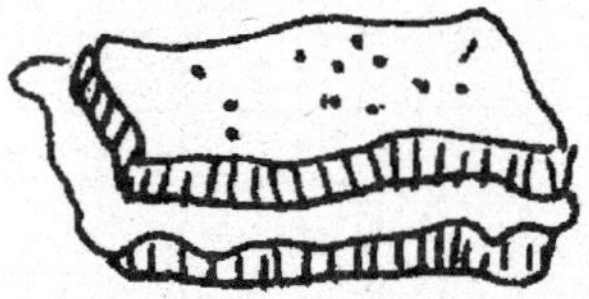	s t r	
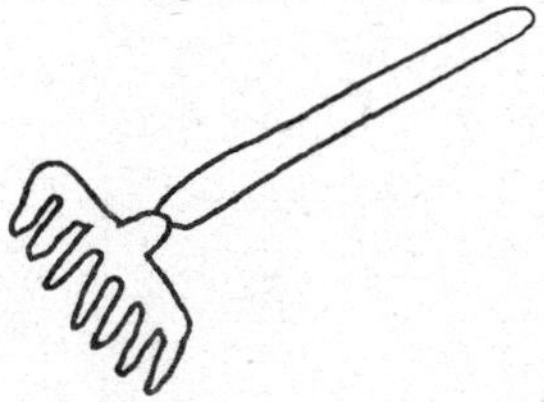	p r k	
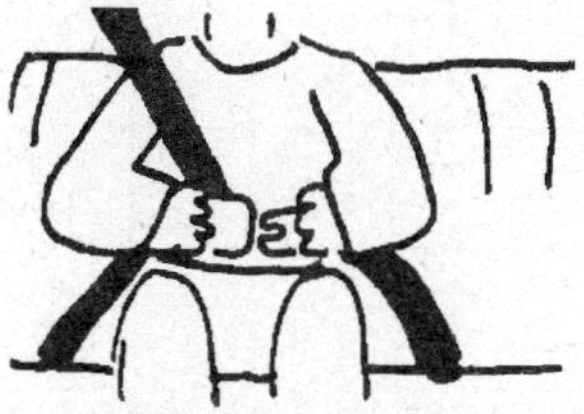	m r s	
	s p f	

Which sound does the word begin with? Write the letter that stands for the sound.

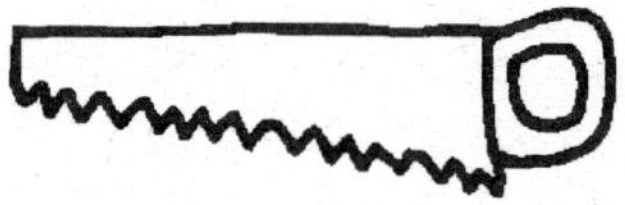

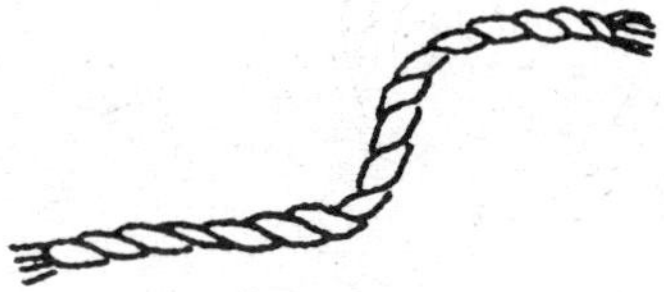

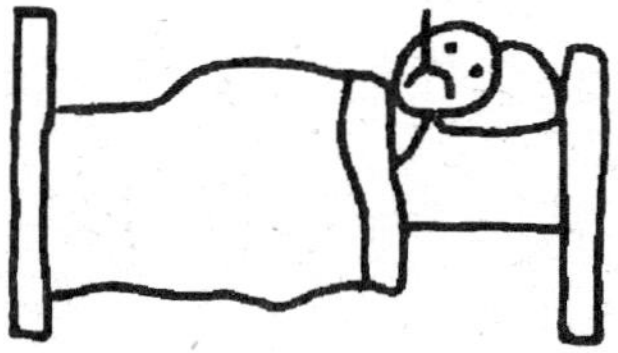

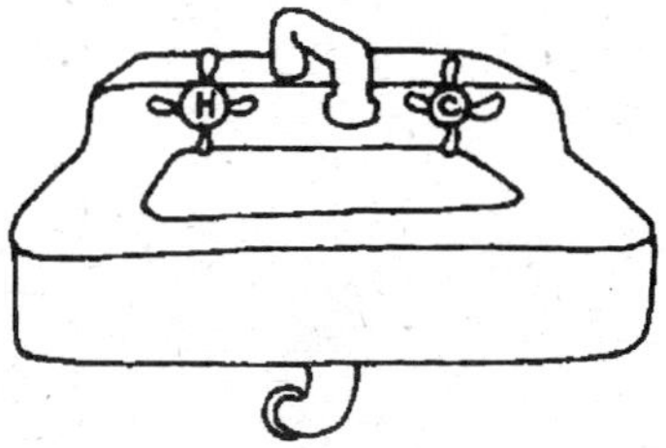

Color or mark the one that is different.

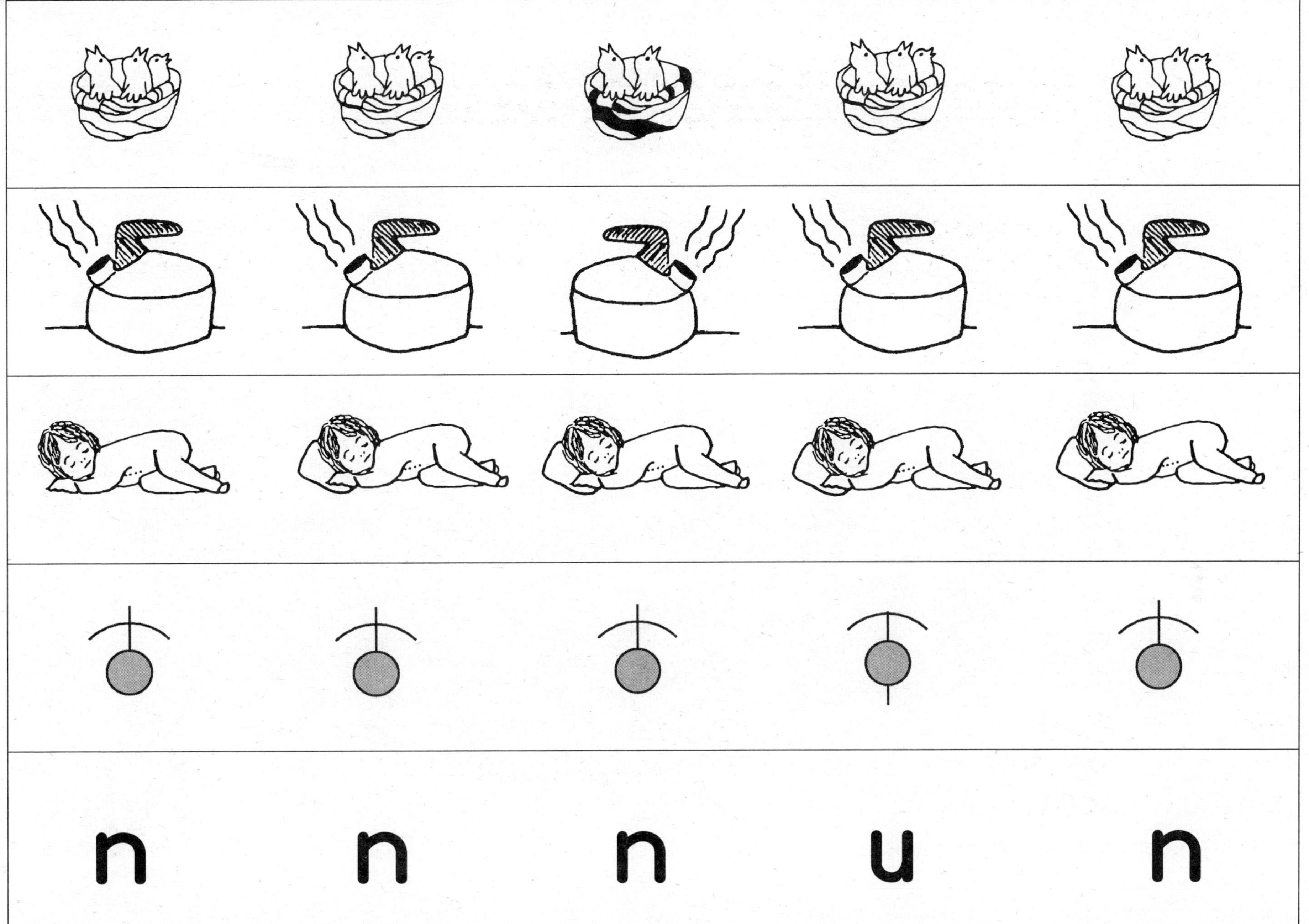

Trace the letter **n** with your finger. This letter has the sound you hear at the beginning of . Say the sound.

n

Capital letters are used
to begin sentences and names.
A capital **n** looks like this: **N.**
Capital letters are two spaces tall.

Nn

Put your pencil on **n**. Follow the path to the picture. Say the sound. Try not to cross any lines.

Teacher: Read the directions aloud while the students listen and work on page 33.

1. I am thinking of something that is used to catch butterflies and sometimes fish or crabs. It has a long handle; a hoop at the end holds a mesh bag. What is it called? [net] Put your finger on the **net.** What sound do you hear at the beginning of **net?** Color the **net** yellow.

2. I am thinking of something people read to learn about the news of the world. Sometimes it has comics in it, too. It is called a ______ [newspaper]. Put your finger on the **newspaper.** What sound do you hear at the beginning of **newspaper?** Put a big X on the **newspaper.**

3. Find something on this page that you wipe your mouth with when you are eating. Sometimes it is made of soft paper and other times it is made of cloth. What is it? [napkin] Put your finger on the **napkin.** What sound do you hear at the beginning of **napkin?** Color the **napkin** your favorite color.

4. I am thinking of something made of metal. It is thin and one end is pointed. You hammer it into two pieces of wood to hold them together. What is it? [nail] Put your finger on the **nail.** What sound does **nail** begin with? Say the sound again. Draw a box around the **nail.**

5. Men may wear one of these when they dress up or go to work. They put it around their neck and tie a knot in it. What is it? [necktie] Put your finger on the **necktie.** What sound does **necktie** begin with? Color the **necktie** red.

6. Now I am thinking of something else people wear around their necks when they dress up. Sometimes it is made of gold or beads. It can have sparkly jewels attached to it. What is it called? [necklace] Put your finger on the **necklace.** What sound do you hear at the beginning of **necklace?** Draw some more jewels on the **necklace.**

7. I am thinking of something that some birds use for their home. They can make it out of grass and weeds; then they lay their eggs in it. What is it? [nest] Put your finger on the **nest.** Say the sound at the beginning of **nest**. Color just the eggs in this **nest.**

8. The last thing is used with thread for sewing. It is long and thin. What is it called? [needle] Put your finger on the **needle.** Say **needle** and the sound you hear at the beginning of it. Draw a circle around the **needle.**

Listen; then follow the directions.

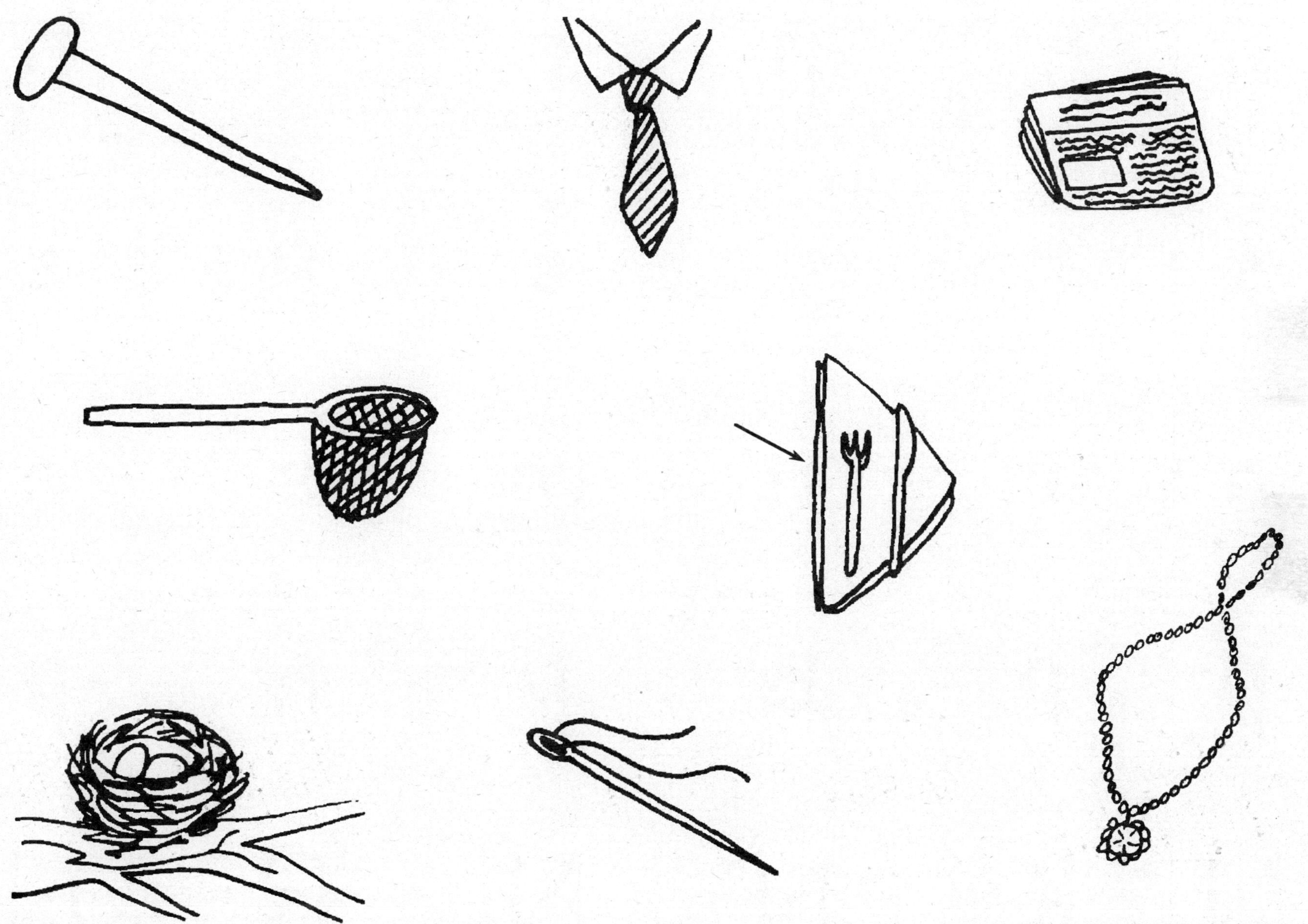

Look carefully at the letter in the box. Circle the letters that match it.

n	m	n	r	n	n
s	n	z	s	p	s
n	r	n	m	s	n
p	p	b	p	n	p
N	K	N	N	R	N

Follow the arrows to write the letter **n**, which says /**n**/as in . Say the sound aloud.

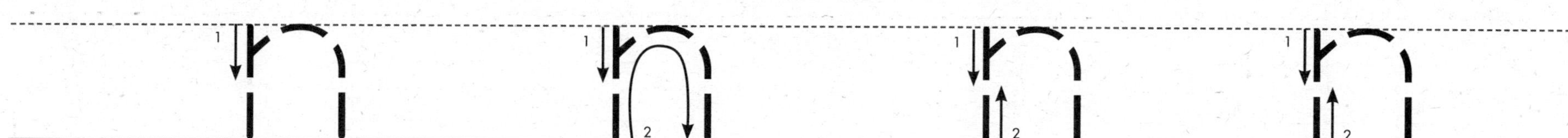

Notice that **n** is only one space tall. Trace the letters.

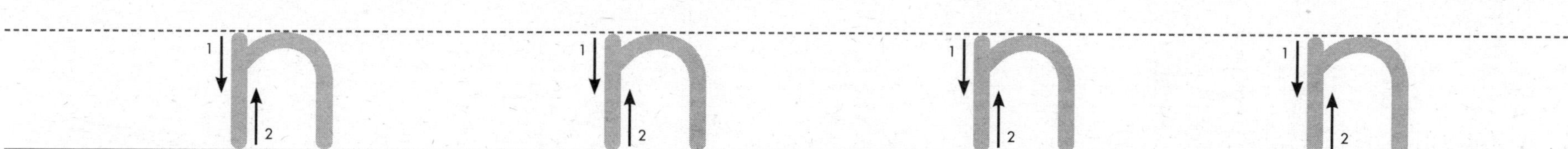

Color each picture whose name begins with **n** as in .

n	 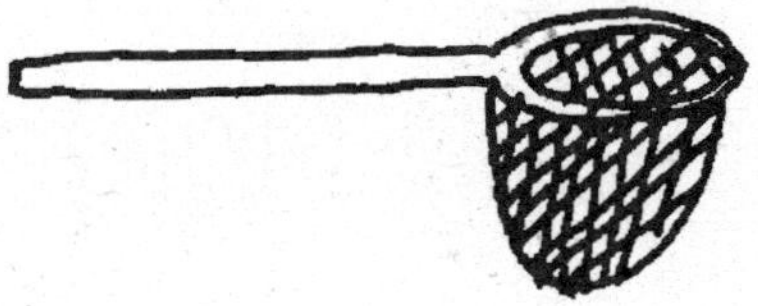	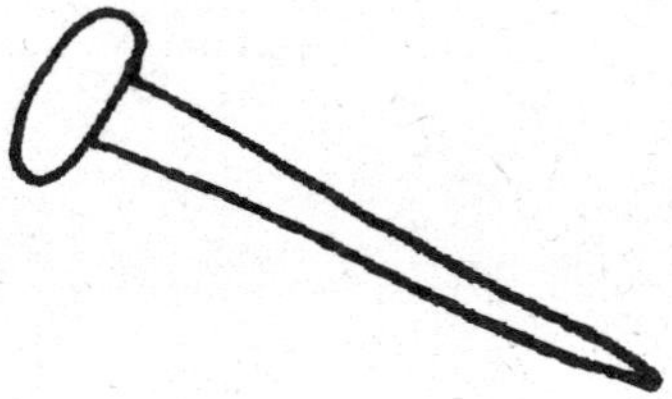 
n	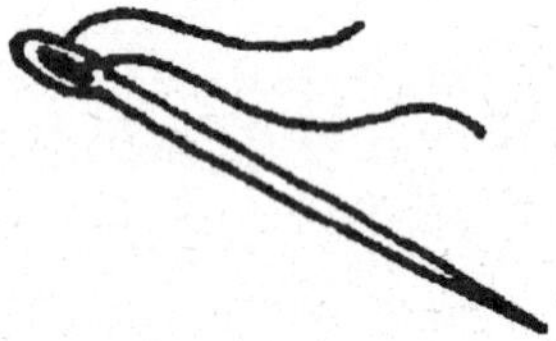 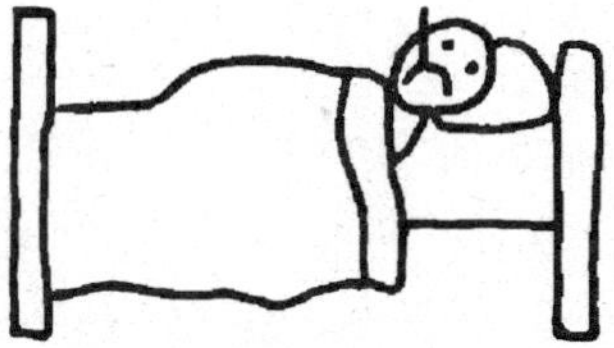	 
n	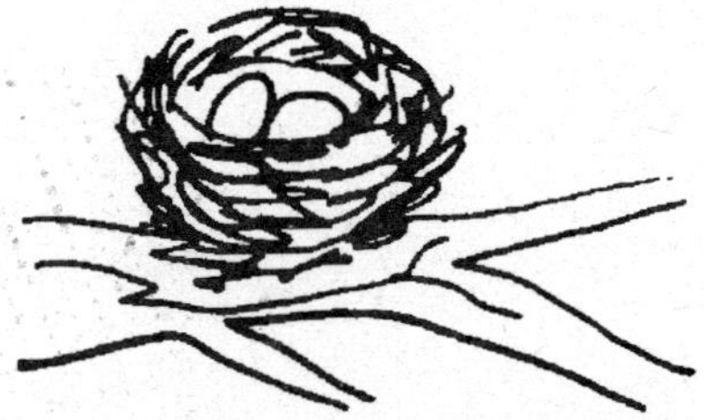 	 

Trace the letters.

n n n n n

Copy the letter.

n

(oval) each picture whose name begins with **n**. Write **n** below those pictures.

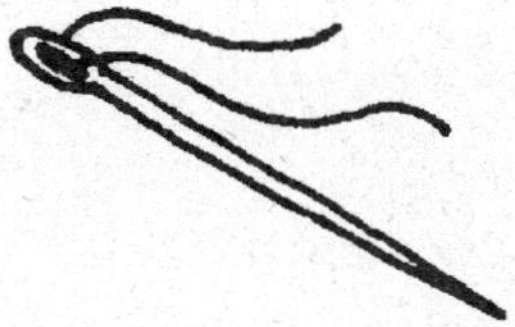

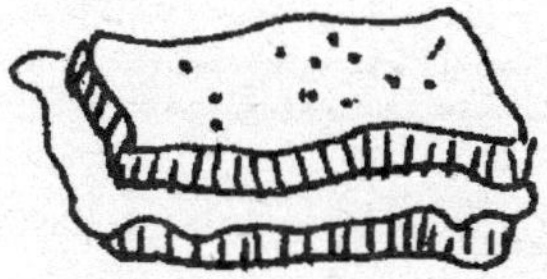

Draw a line from each picture to the letter that begins its name.

Say the name of the picture and the sound of its first letter.	Find the letter. Circle it.	Write the letter.
	p b t	
	s n k	
	r p m	
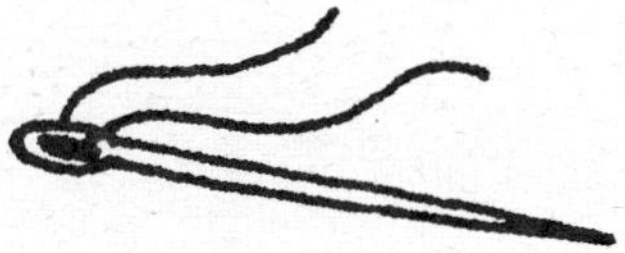	n f p	
	b t s	

Which sound does the word begin with? Write the letter that stands for the sound.

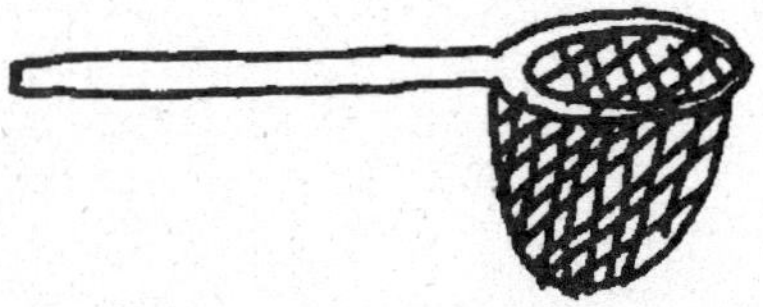

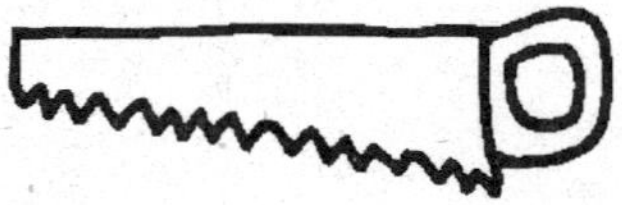

Color or mark the one that is different.

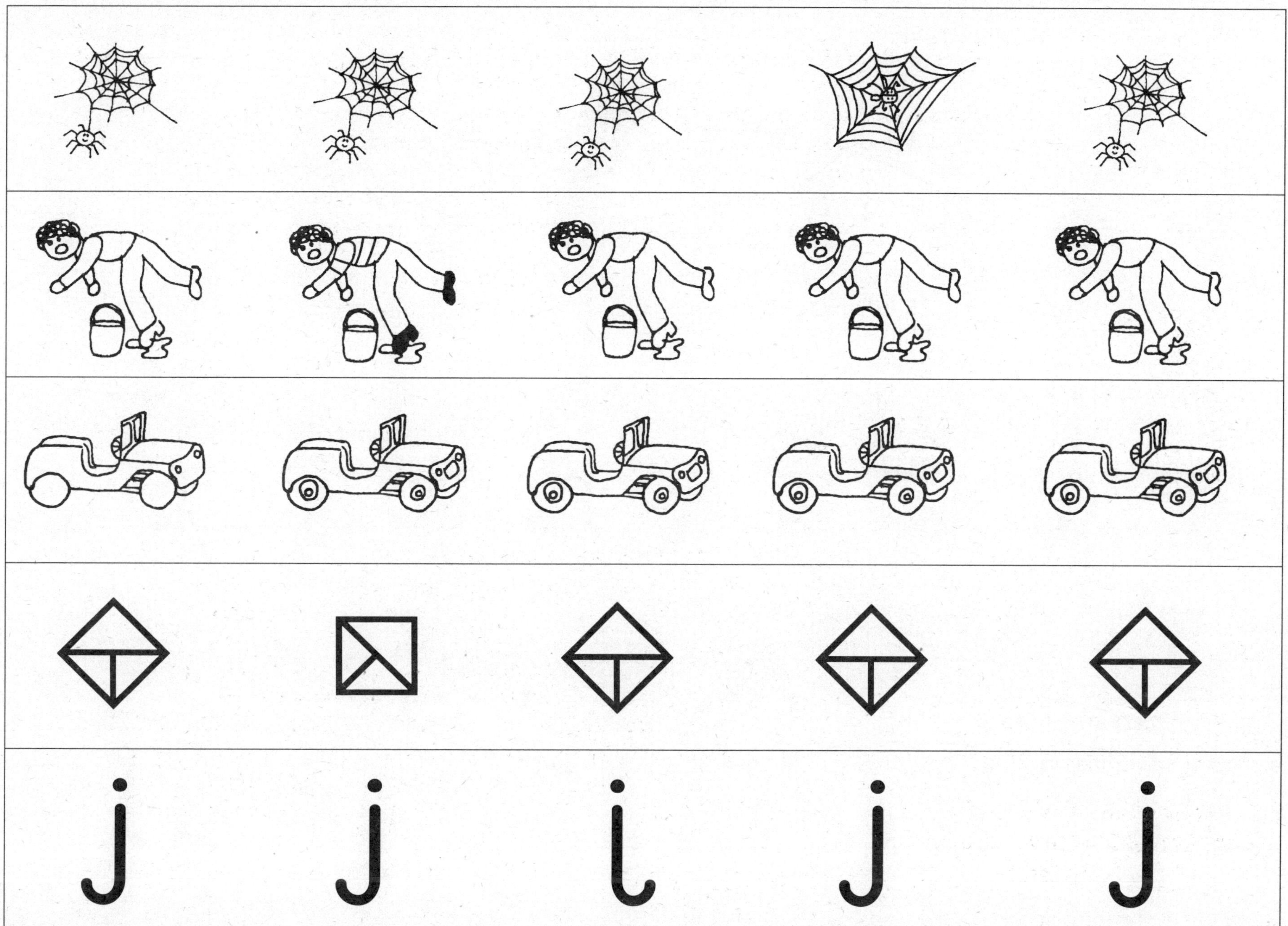

Trace the letter j with your finger. This letter has the sound you hear at the beginning of . Say the sound.

2

1

Capital letters are used
to begin sentences and names.
A capital j looks like this: J.
Capital letters are two spaces tall.

Jj

Put your pencil on **j**. Follow the path to the picture. Say the sound. Try not to cross any lines.

Teacher: Read the directions aloud while the students listen and work on page 45.

1. I am thinking of something you wear when it is cool. It covers the top half of your body and keeps you warm if you button it. What is it? [jacket] Put your finger on the **jacket.** What sound does **jacket** begin with? Color the **jacket** any way you want.

2. Find a picture of something you can do with a rope. It is fun and good exercise. It is called _____ rope [jumping]. Put your finger on the girl **jumping** rope. Do you like to **jump** rope? What sound do you hear at the beginning of **jump?** Draw some grass for the girl to **jump** on.

3. This is a pumpkin with a face carved in it for Halloween. Sometimes you put a light inside. Now it is called a _____ [jack-o'-lantern]. Put your finger on the **jack-o'-lantern.** What sound does **jack-o'-lantern** start with? Carefully color the **jack-o'-lantern.**

4. I am thinking of what you spread on toast. It is sweet and tasty and made from fruit. It comes in a jar. What do you call it? [jam, jelly] Either **jam** or **jelly** is a good answer. Put your finger on the **jam** or **jelly.** What sound do **jam** and **jelly** begin with? Draw a box around the jar of **jam.**

5. When you toss several balls in the air and keep catching them without dropping them, it is called _____ [juggling]. Put your finger on the picture for **juggle.** Have you ever tried to **juggle?** What sound does **juggling** begin with? Draw another ball for the juggler.

6. I am thinking of something found on a playground. It is fun to climb, swing from, and jump off one of these. Its name begins with the sound of /j/. What is it called? [jungle gym] Put your finger on the **jungle gym.** Say the sound you hear at the beginning of **jungle gym.** Add something to the **jungle gym.** Color it to make it look nice.

7. The next picture is of a toy that pops out of a box. Sometimes you turn a handle until the lid springs open. What do we call it? [jack-in-the-box] Put your finger on the **jack-in-the-box.** How many of you have seen a **jack-in-the-box?** They are lots of fun. What sound do you hear at the beginning of **jack-in-the-box?** Color the box, but not Jack!

8. The last picture shows a container that milk, cider, or syrup comes in. What is its name? [jug] Have you heard of a **jug?** Put your finger on the **jug.** Say **jug** and the sound you hear at the beginning of **jug.** Put an X on it.

Listen; then follow the directions.

Draw a line from the box to each picture whose name begins with /j/ as in .

j

Follow the arrows to write the letter **j**, which says /**j**/as in  . Say the sound aloud.

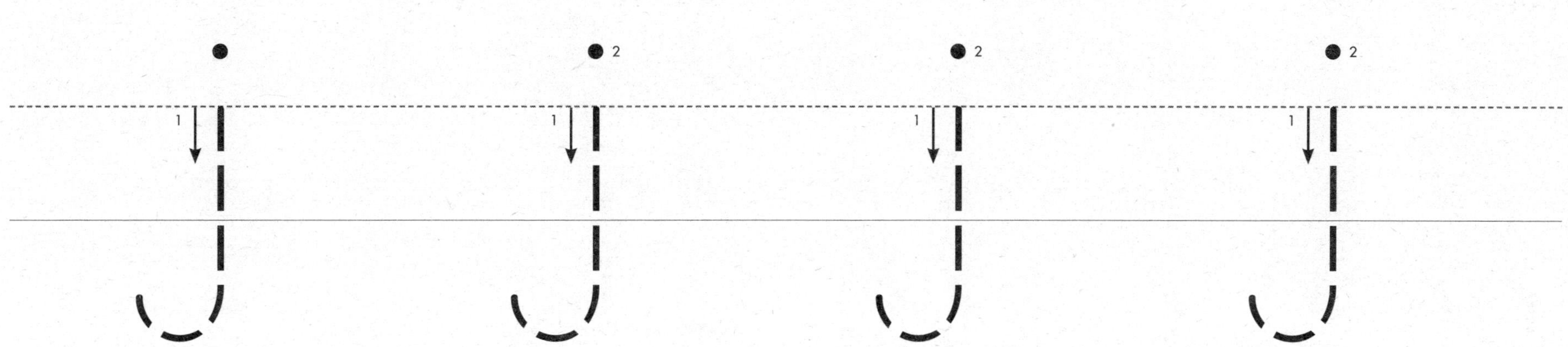

Notice that **j** hangs below the line like **p**. Trace the letters.

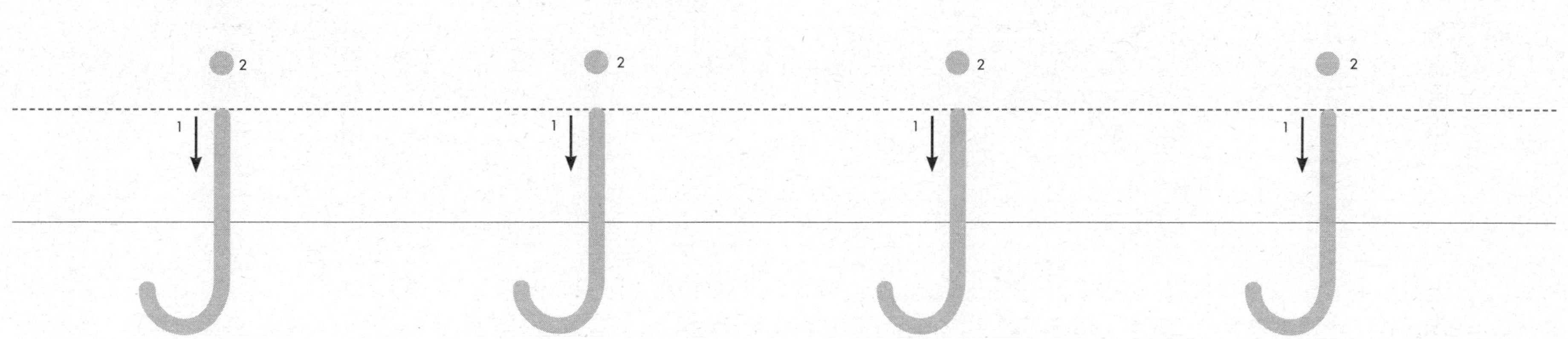

j says /j/ as in [jack-o'-lantern]. On each line color the picture whose name begins with /j/.

j

j

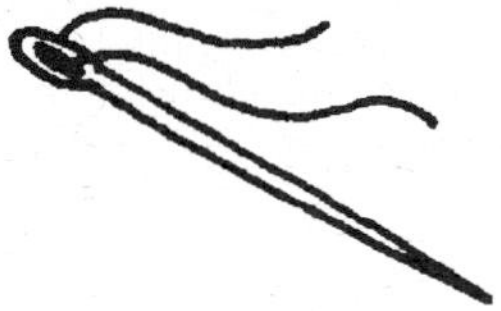

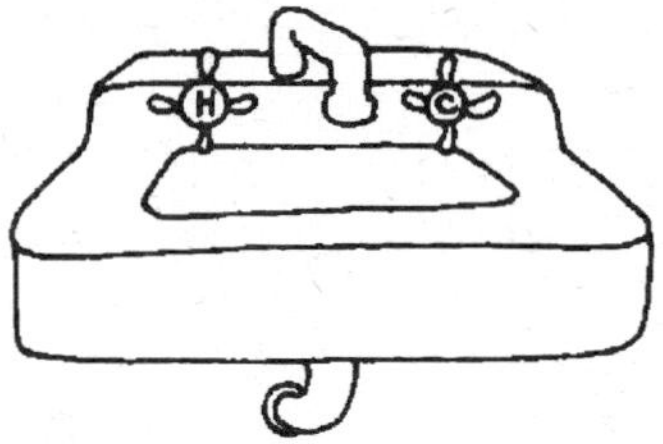

j

JAM

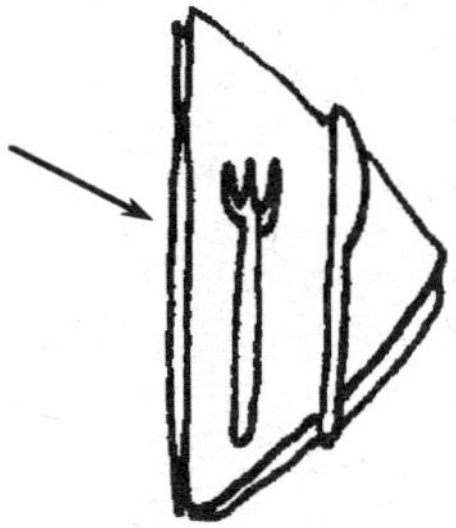

j

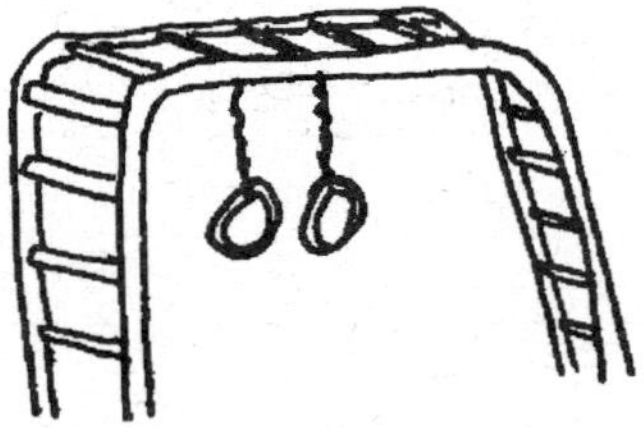

j

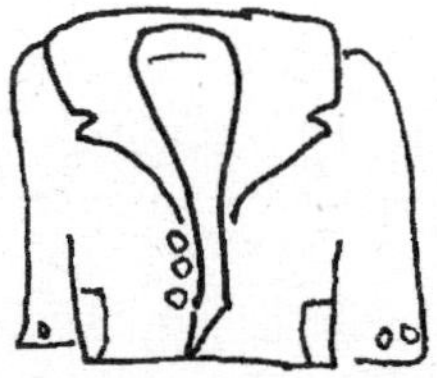

Trace the letters.

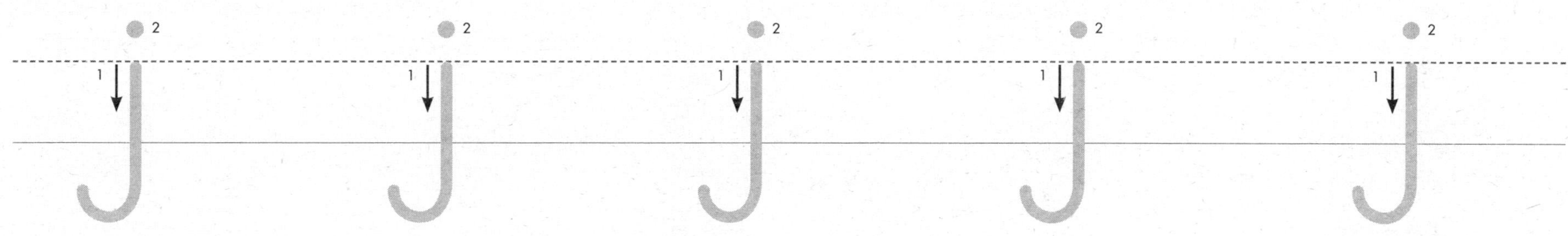

Copy the letter.

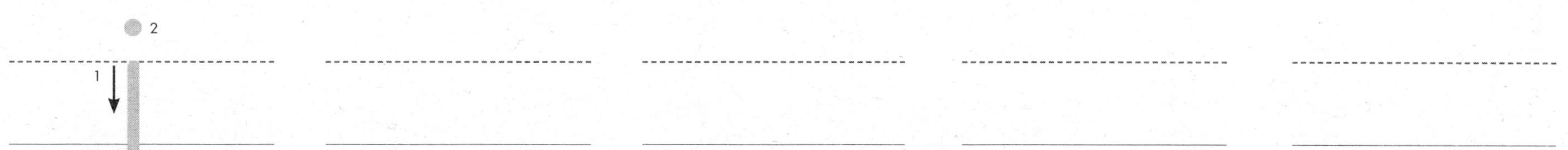

◯ each picture whose name begins with j. Write j below those pictures.

What letter does the picture's name begin with? Circle it.

Say the name of the picture and the sound of its first letter.	Find the letter. Circle it.	Write the letter.
	s j n	
	r t j	
	s p f	
	j m n	
	p j r	

Which sound does the word begin with? Write the letter that stands for the sound.

Color or mark the one that is different.

Trace the letter **h** with your finger. This letter has the sound you hear at the beginning of  . Say the sound.

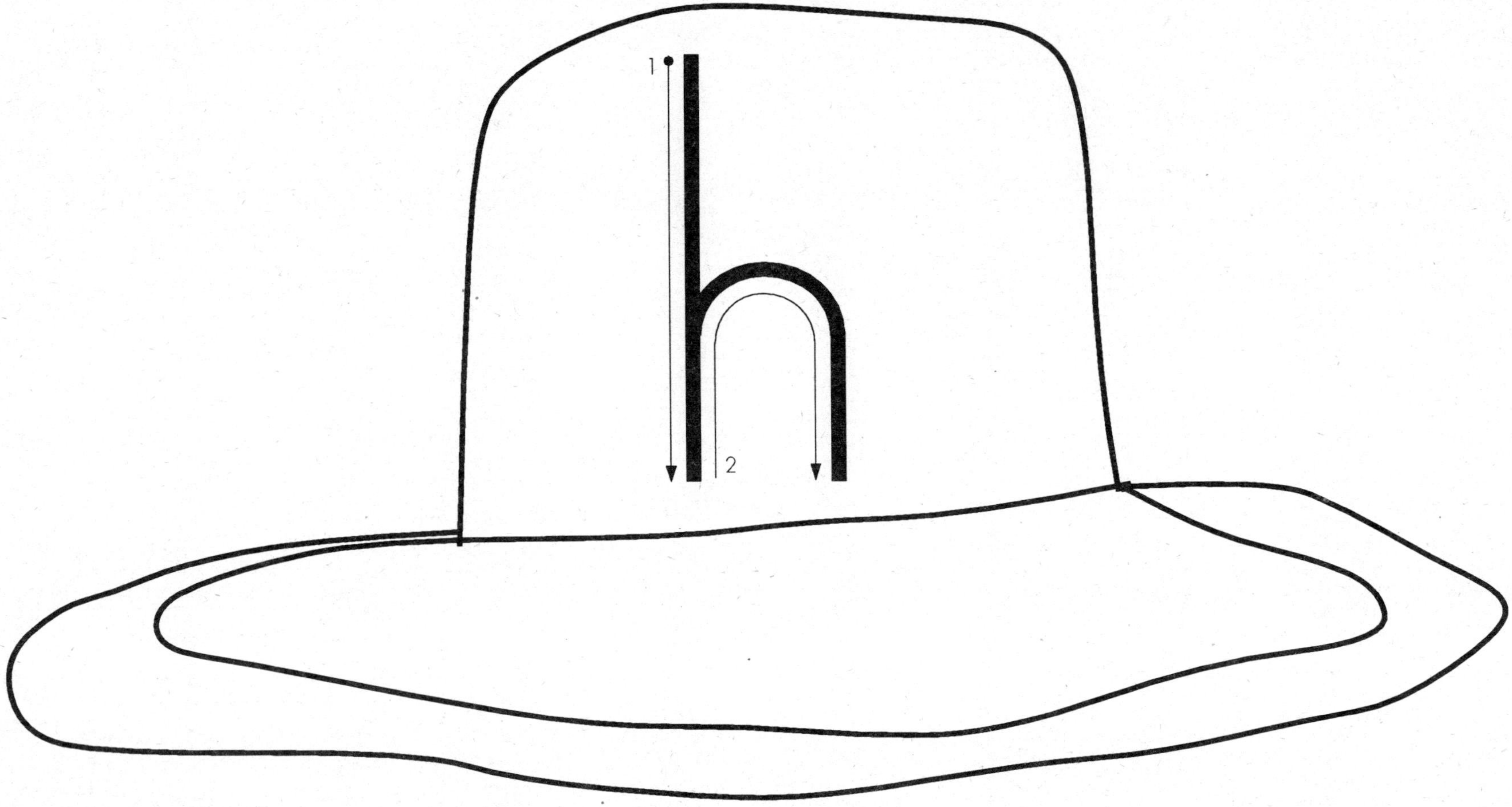

Capital letters are used
to begin sentences and names.
A capital **h** looks like this: H.
Capital letters are two spaces tall.

Put your pencil on **h.** Follow the path to the picture. Try not to cross any lines.

Look carefully at the letter in the box. Circle the letters that match it.

h	h	b	h	n	h
n	n	r	n	n	m
h	n	h	m	h	n
j	h	j	p	j	j
H	N	H	H	F	H

Draw a line from each hat to the letter **hat** begins with.

Teacher: Read the directions aloud while the students listen and work on page 59.

1. I am thinking of something that tastes good. It has a bun around it and is fun to eat at a baseball game. What is it? [hot dog] Put your finger on the **hot dog.** What sound does **hot dog** begin with? Draw a box around the **hot dog.**

2. I am thinking of a part of your body that is attached to your arm. You use it nearly every time you do something. It has fingers and a thumb. What is it? [hand] Put your finger on the **hand.** What sound do you hear at the beginning of **hand?** Find the **hand** and draw a ring on one of the fingers.

3. I am thinking of something you hang your clothes on in a closet. It is made of wire or plastic. What is it? [hanger] Put your finger on the **hangers.** Say the sound you hear at the beginning of **hanger.** Draw an X on the **hangers.**

4. You can use this tool to pound nails into wood. It has a wooden handle and a metal head. What is it? [hammer] Put your finger on the **hammer.** Can you hear the /h/ sound at the beginning of **hammer?** Say it. Color the head of the **hammer.**

5. I am thinking of something people live in. It has doors, windows, a roof, and sometimes a chimney. What is it? [house] Put your finger on the **house.** What sound does **house** begin with? Draw a path up to the front door and color the **house.**

6. This is something that makes a loud noise. Cars always have one. Sometimes bikes have one, too. What do you call it? [horn] Put your finger on the **horn.** Say the sound at the beginning of **horn.** Draw a circle around the **horn.**

7. Find something you can wear on your head to keep the sun or rain off. What is its name? [hat] Put your finger on the **hat.** What sound do you hear at the beginning of **hat?** Draw a person wearing this **hat.**

8. I am thinking of a big animal with four legs. It can run fast. You can sometimes ride on its back or hitch it to a wagon. What is the name of this animal? [horse] Put your finger on the **horse.** What sound does **horse** begin with? Color the **horse.**

Listen; then follow the directions.

Color each picture whose name begins with **h** as in hat.

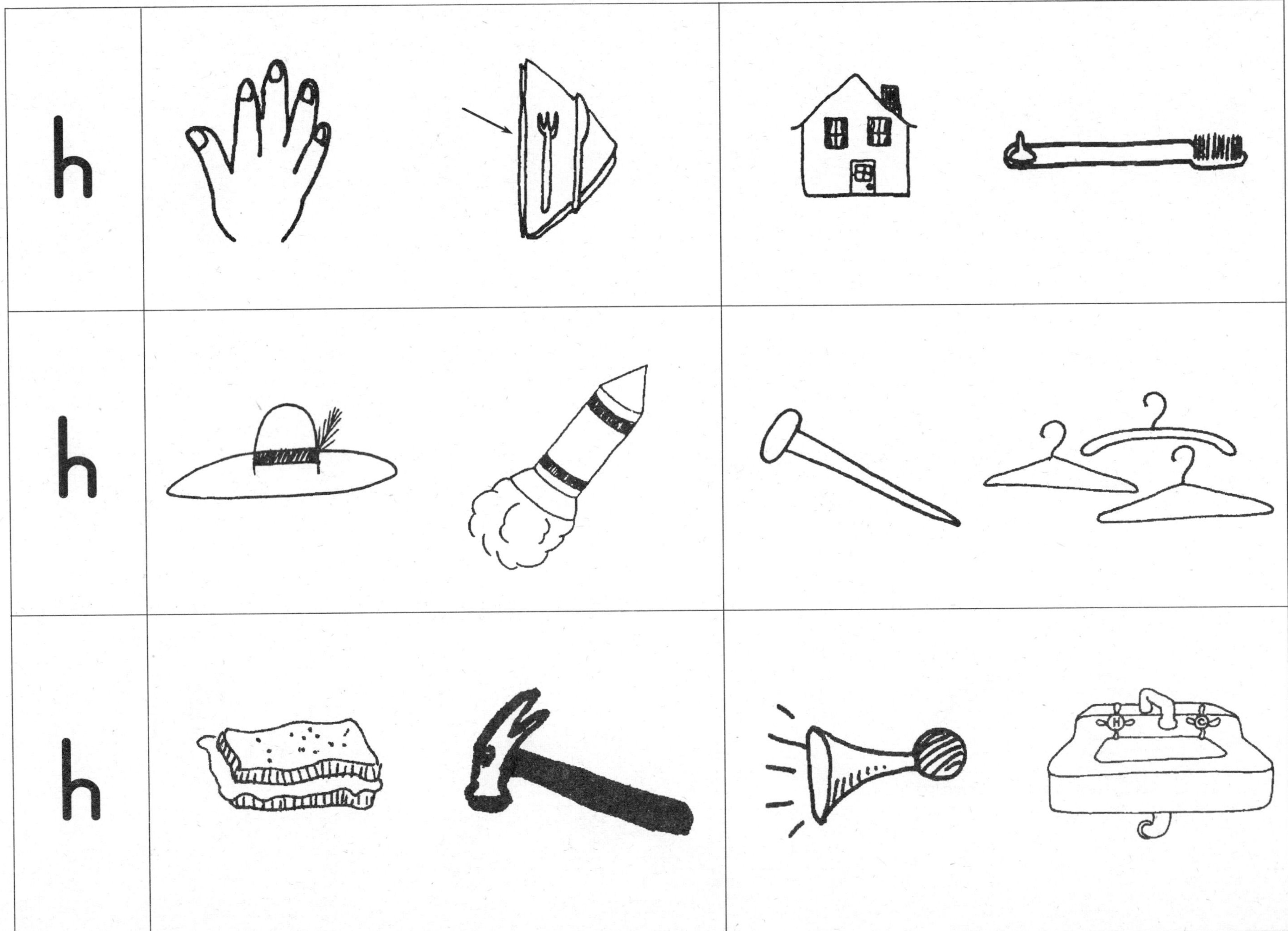

Follow the arrows to write the letter **h**, which says /**h**/as in hat. Say the sound aloud.

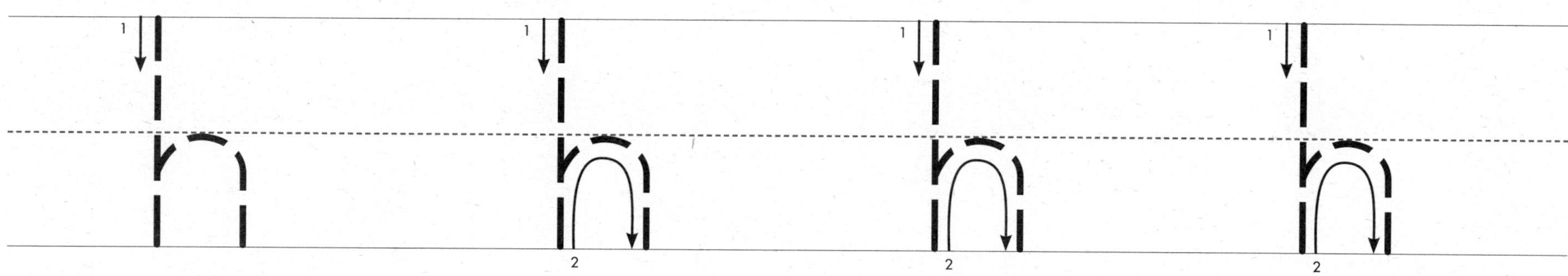

Notice that **h** is two spaces tall. Trace the letters.

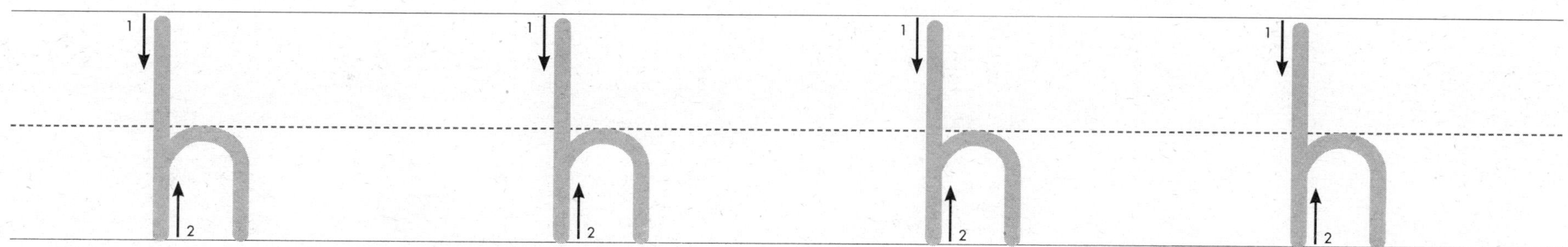

Say the sound of each letter. Then color the picture whose name begins with that sound.

Trace the letters.

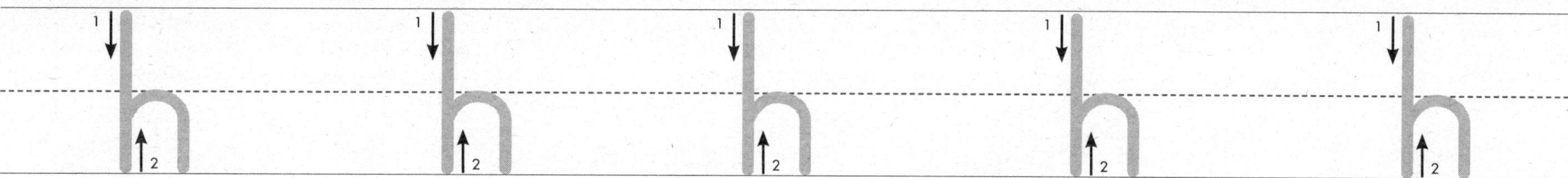

Copy the letter.

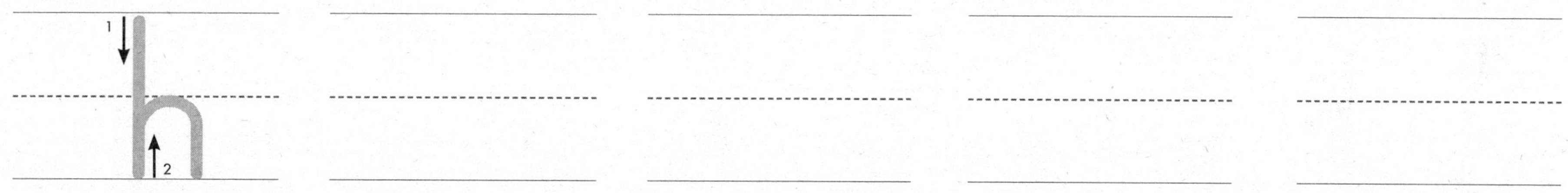

◯ each letter whose name begins with **h**. Write **h** below those pictures.

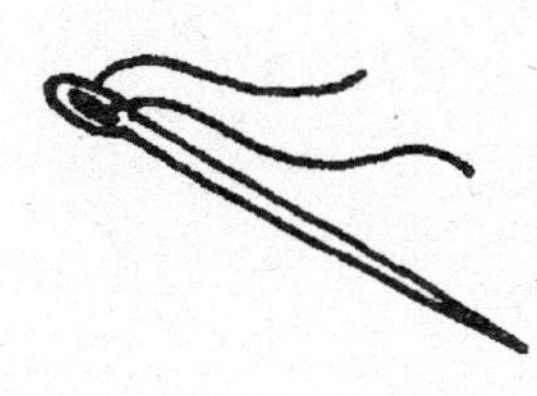

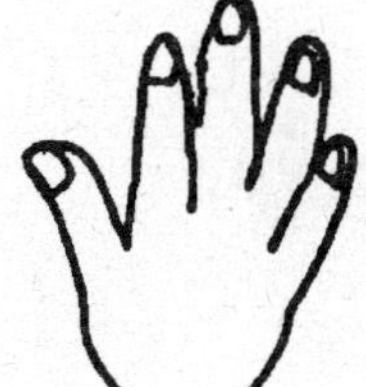

Which letter does the picture's name begin with? Circle it.

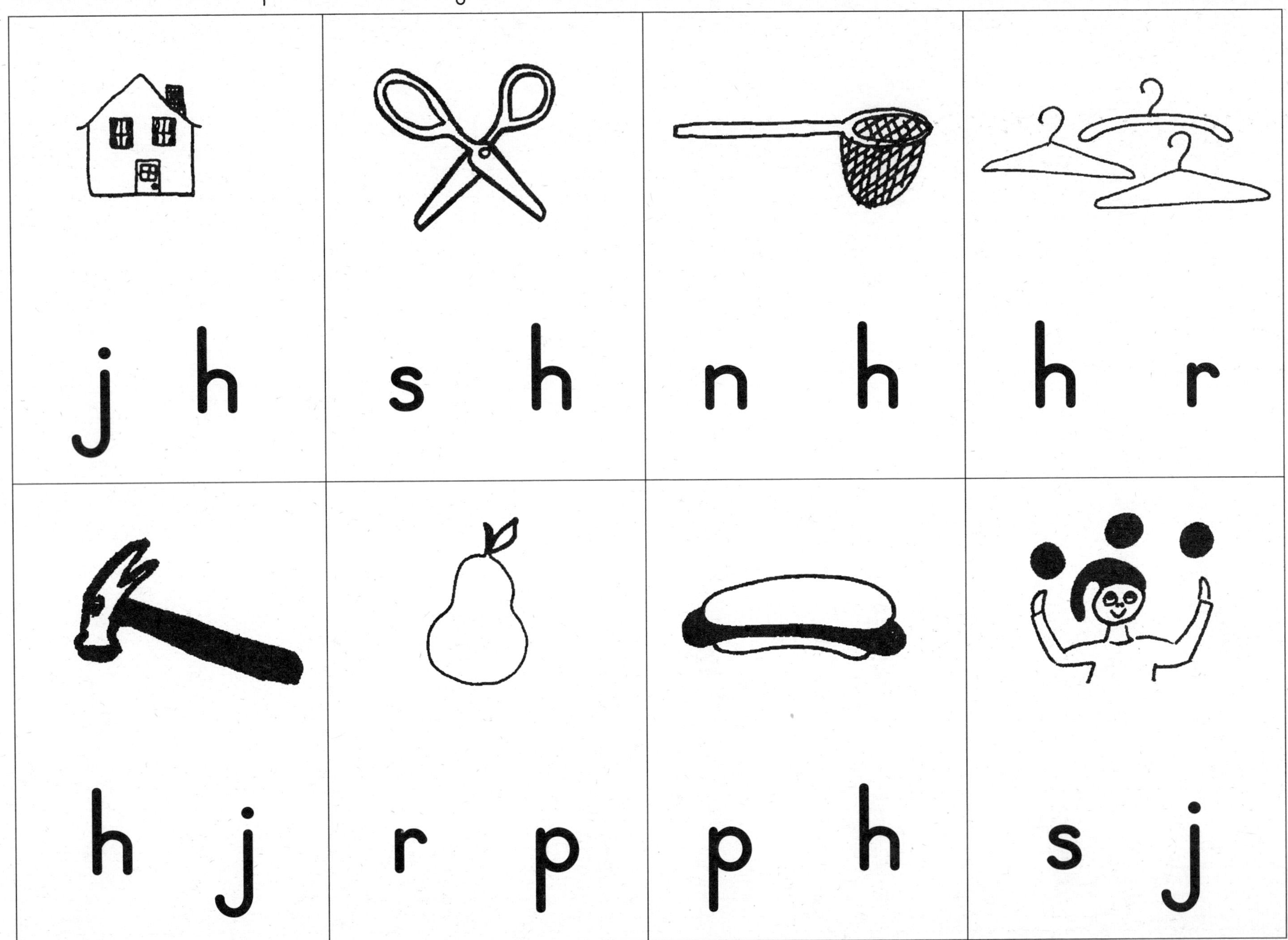

Say the name of the picture and the sound of its first letter.	Find the letter. Circle it.			Write the letter.
	n	h	j	
	f	r	t	
	b	j	h	
	n	b	m	
	j	b	p	

Which sound does the word begin with? Write the letter that stands for the sound.

Color or mark the one that is different.

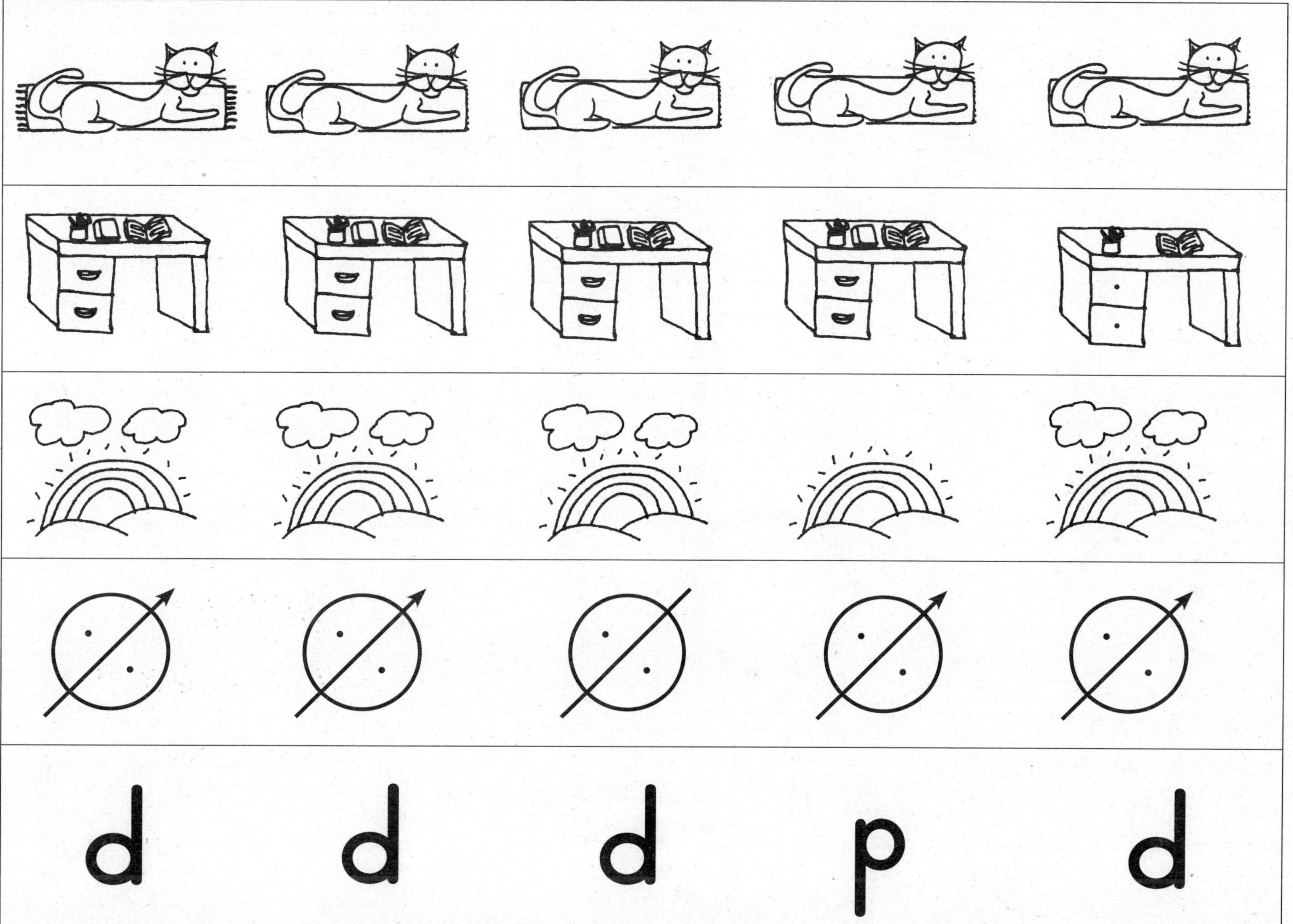

Trace the letter **d** with your finger. This letter has the sound you hear at the beginning of [duck picture]. Say the sound.

Capital letters are used
to begin sentences and names.
A capital **d** looks like this: D.
Capital letters are two spaces tall.

Dd

Put your pencil on **d.** Follow the path to the picture. Try not to cross any lines.

Teacher: Read the directions aloud while the students listen and work on page 71.

1. I am thinking of an animal that makes a quacking sound. It can swim on a pond. What is it? [duck] Put your finger on the **duck.** What sound does **duck** begin with? Color the water blue and the **duck** any color you wish.

2. I am thinking of an animal that is playful and fun. It wags its tail when it likes you. Sometimes it barks. What is it called? [dog] Put your finger on the **dog.** Say the sound at the beginning of **dog.** Draw a leash on the **dog.**

3. I am thinking of something that lived a long time ago. It was very large. This prehistoric animal was one of the first creatures on earth. What is it? [dinosaur] Put your finger on the **dinosaur.** Say the sound at the beginning of **dinosaur.** Draw a box around the **dinosaur.**

4. I am thinking of a toy that looks like a baby but is not real. It is fun to play with. You can dress it up in clothes. What is it called? [doll] Put your finger on the **doll.** What sound does **doll** begin with? Color the **doll** any way you like.

5. Find something you might use to play board games. You shake them and throw them down so you can count the dots on top. What are these called? [dice] Put your finger on the **dice.** Have you ever seen **dice?** What sound does **dice** start with? Draw a circle around the **dice.**

6. If you jump off a high board with your arms out straight and go head first into the water, it is called a ____ [dive]. Put your finger on the picture of the person **diving.** Learning to **dive** takes a lot of practice in deep water. Say the sound you hear at the beginning of **dive.** Color the water blue or green.

7. I am thinking of something you put food on. When you finish eating from it, you must wash the _____ [dish]. Put your finger on the **dish.** What sound do you hear at the beginning of **dish?** Draw some food in the **dish.**

8. The last picture shows a girl making deep holes in the ground with a shovel. What is she doing? [digging] Put your finger on the picture of the girl **digging.** What sound does **dig** begin with? Draw an X on the girl who is **digging.**

Listen; then follow the directions.

d says /**d**/ as in duck. On each line color the picture whose name begins with /**d**/.

Follow the arrows to write the letter **d,** which says /**d**/ as in duck. Say the sound aloud.

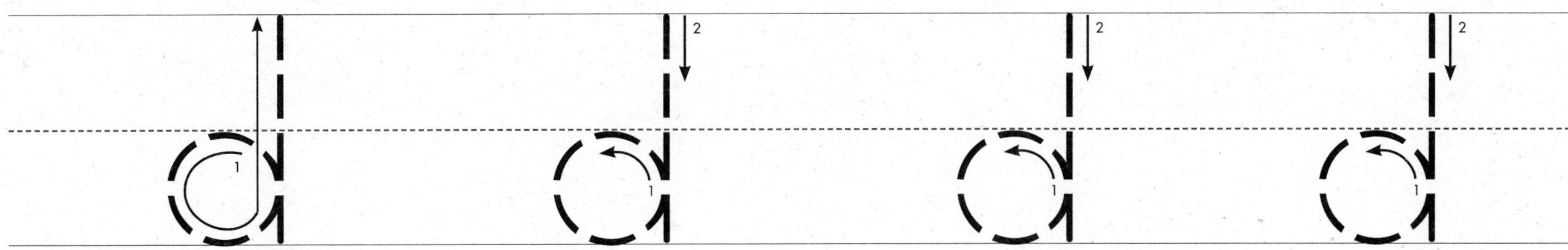

Trace the letters.

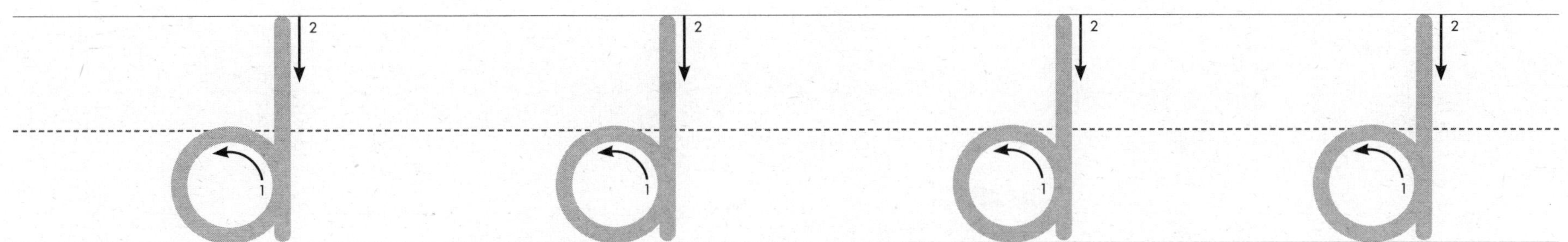

Draw a line from the tag to each picture whose name begins with /**d**/ as in [duck picture].

Trace the letters.

d d d d d

Copy the letter.

d

( ) each letter whose name begins with **d.** Write **d** below those pictures.

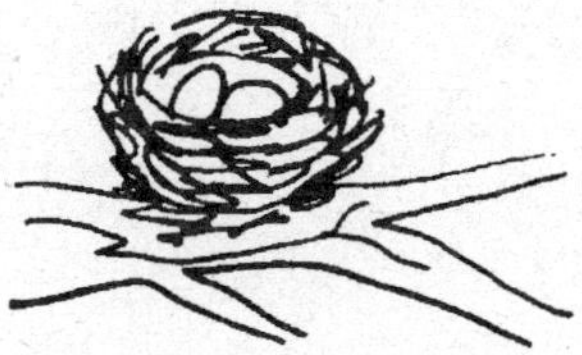

Which letter does the picture's name begin with? Circle it.

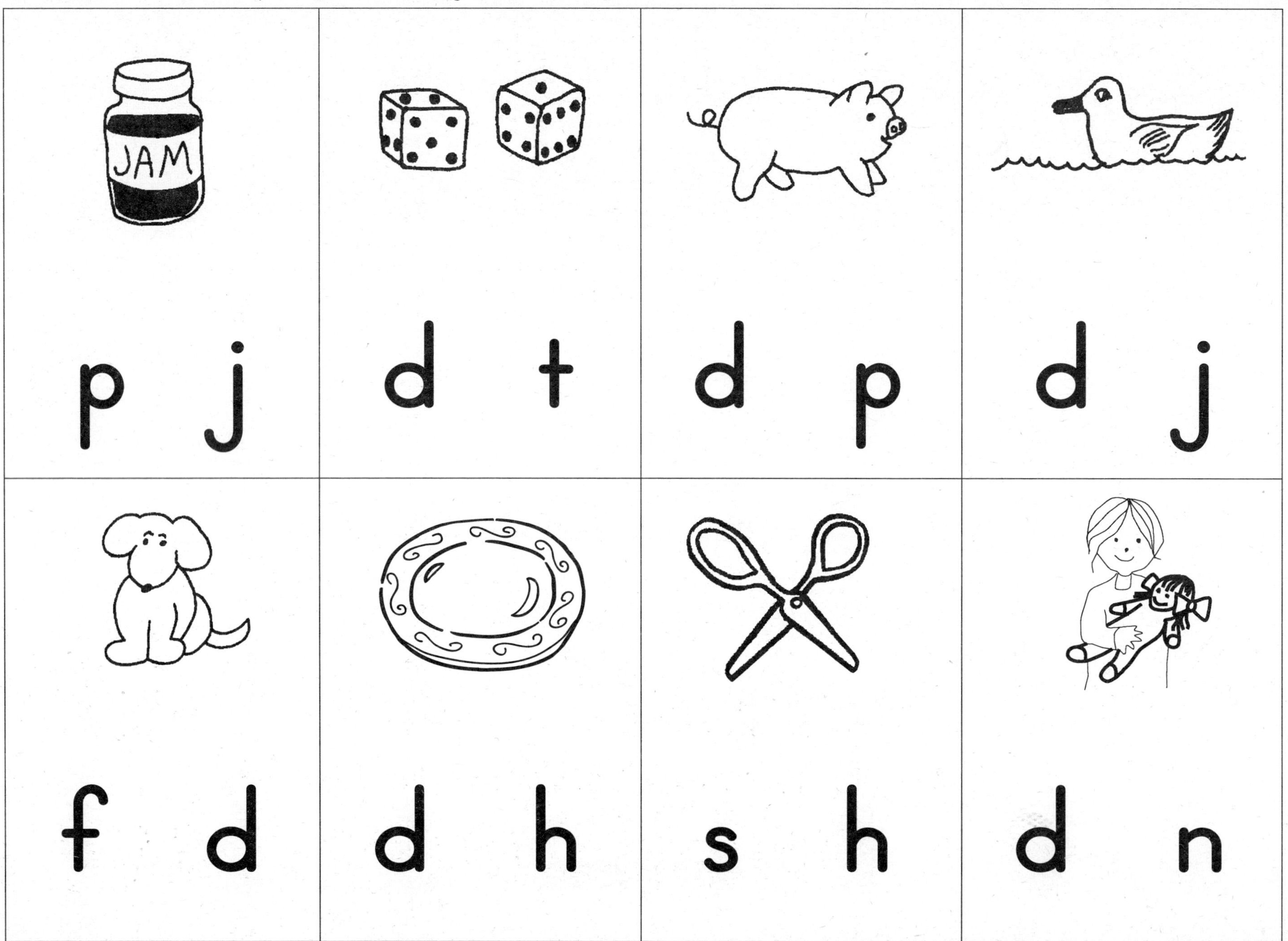

Name the pictures in each row. Which sound do the words begin with? Write the letter that stands for that sound.

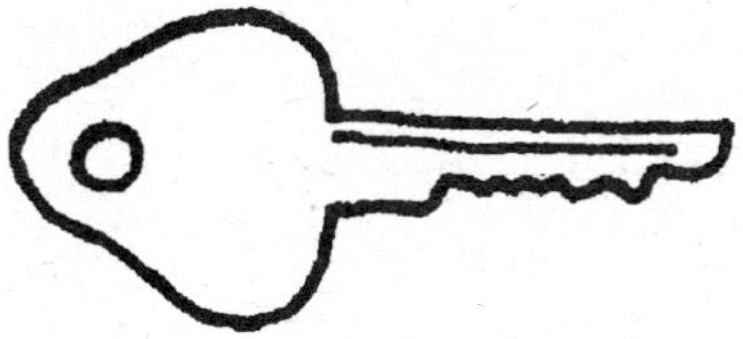		

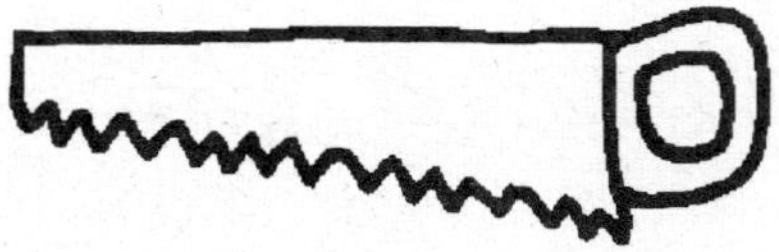		
	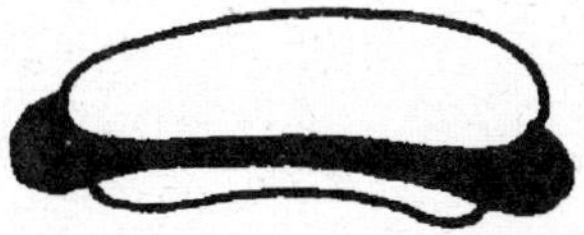	

Which sound does the word begin with? Write the letter that stands for the sound.